The Modern Machiavelli

Playing Office Politics to Win

Copyright © 2020

All rights reserved. This book or any portion thereof may not be reproduced or used in any manner whatsoever without the express written permission of the author.

Foreword

There are many people out there who claim that office politics is a waste of time. That success comes from focusing on your job and doing it well. That talent will rise to the top without help.

These people are, to put it politely, losers.

Losers who are doomed to be left behind in the dirt, while those who *are* good at politics cruise past them on their way to meaningful jobs with real salaries.

If you want to succeed, if you want to grow your career and move onto *good* projects and have *any* chance whatsoever of influencing the company around you… then you need to learn the art of office politics.

Luckily, this book is here to help you out. There is no discussion of morality, no introspection as to whether office politics is really necessary in the modern workplace. Instead we focus on clear, rational advice so that you can achieve your goals via influencing others. This book is divided into multiple chapters, each of which covers a different aspect of developing and using your political skills.

- Chapter 1 (page 7) **introduces** the world of office politics and the associated requirements.
- Chapter 2 (page 11) discusses **power in the workplace** – sources of power, the distinction between formal and informal power, and the chapters you need to read based on your current situation.
- Chapter 3 (page 21) covers the **essential skills** which are necessary to support any attempt at persuading others or utilising office politics in your plans.
- Chapter 4 (page 33) is devoted to **fundamentals** and the way they relate to your current situation. It provides hints on decoding your own values, political skill and style, and the organisation which you are a part of.
- Chapter 5 (page 44) looks at **initial impressions**. It covers the importance of making a competent first impression, tailoring your style to match workplace reputation, and offers hints on fine-tuning external appearance towards professionalism.
- Chapter 6 (page 57) is about creating and maintaining a **competent reputation**. We look at baseline expectations, moving beyond

these, and the surprising benefits you have from being good at meetings.
- Chapter 7 (page 76) involves the art of making and selling **good decisions**, an essential skill for those who wish to progress upwards in the company
- Chapter 8 (page 92) is focused on the **fundamentals of communication** and their impact on office politics – from basic skills and selling ideas through to dealing with or using 'no' and holding tough conversations with others.
- Chapter 9 (page 119) is about **managing upwards** – to your manager and above. It includes typical manager requirements, dealing with new managers, and a short guide to detecting managerial insanity.
- Chapter 10 (page 129) is all about **managing downwards** – developing a leadership personality, making the most of your team, taking over a new team, and moving unwanted people on.
- Chapter 11 (page 145) looks at **networks**. It covers creating, maintaining, and tracking networks for professional development.
- Chapter 12 (page 155) is about **influencing others**, whether it be picking targets, identifying tradeable currencies, using a suitable strategy, or simply noting typical mistakes newcomers make.
- Chapter 13 (page 171) looks at **negotiation**. The approach outlined here is as applicable to formal negotiations as it is for quick back-and-forth discussions over a conspiratorial cup of coffee.
- Chapter 14 (page 194) is for when **things are going wrong**. It examines last-ditch methods for achieving success as well as effective approaches to cover your arse when they inevitably fail.
- Chapter 15 (page 200) is all about **moving on**. It covers the decision to move onwards, the art of negotiation for your new role, and a set of tell-tale signs that firings and lay-offs are coming in.
- Finally Chapter 16 (page 209) provides a summary of **typical political shenanigans** which you will encounter and (most likely) try to use on other colleagues. It includes helpful tips for defending or attacking with these methods.

Ready to learn? Then read on.

Table of contents

Foreword 2
Table of contents 4
1. Introduction 7
2. Power in the workplace 11
    What is formal and informal power? 11
    Sources of power 12
    Using power, sensibly 17
3. Political skills to develop 21
    Acting 21
    Mimicry 22
    Flattery 25
    Trading favours 26
    Assertiveness 28
    Self-promotion 29
    Networking 30
    Actively building a reputation 31
4. Understand your current situation 33
    Understanding yourself 34
    Understanding your organisation 40
5. Managing initial impressions 44
    The importance of first impressions 44
    Dressing to match expectations 48
    Appearance matters 52
    Shaking hands 55
6. Creating a competent reputation 57
    What are the baseline expectations? 57
    Moving beyond the baseline 61
    Managing your time 68

Table of contents

- Being efficient with meetings 69
- 7. Become known as a decision-maker 76
  - Questions to ask yourself 76
  - The decision-making process 81
  - Persuading others that you've made the right decision 87
- 8. Interacting with others 92
  - Communication basics 92
  - Interacting with your colleagues 102
  - Getting your ideas across 105
  - Saying no to others 108
  - Others saying no to you 111
  - Tough Discussions 113
- 9. Dealing with managers 119
  - Dealing with a new manager 121
  - Gaining control as a weak player 123
  - Detecting insane managers 125
- 10. Dealing with subordinates 129
  - What do you need to succeed? 129
  - Developing your leadership personality 130
  - Making the most of your team 132
  - Starting with a new team 140
  - When people want, or need, to go 142
- 11. Building and using a network 145
  - Creating networks 145
  - Keep track of your network 149
  - Nurture your network 150
  - Entertaining others 151
- 12. Influencing others 155
  - Always plan first 155

Choose who you will target 156
What 'currency' is in play? 159
Trading back and forth 162
You have more influence than you think 165
Tailor your discussion to their personality 167

13. Negotiation 171
Basics of negotiating 171
Factors to determine before you start 174
The first offer 180
Offer and counteroffer 185
The best and final offer 190

14. Risky situations 194
Be flexible 194
Try one last push for success 194
Cover your arse 196

15. Moving to a new role 200
Moving upwards 200
The interview process 201
Negotiating pay and promotion 203
Starting at the new job 204
Lay-offs 206

16. Typical political shenanigans 209
Daily occurrences 209
Nasty betrayals 218
Career-killers 226

17. Appendix: Further reading 229

1. Introduction

The most important thing to remember when reading this book is that politics comes from human nature – we've been playing games in an attempt to get power for many thousands of years, we'll undoubtedly be doing the same several thousand years from now. This means that if you want to achieve anything *useful* in life, anything which involves success in society or with the help of others, then you need to understand politics. You can certainly ignore it for a while, you can ignore *anything* for a while. But this is relying on luck to develop your career – and luck will eventually run out.

Why is it so important? It all comes down to the source of office politics, which is all about *power*. Gaining power, using power, distributing power, anything you can think of. Power can come in all forms, so we'll use a fairly broad definition here: Power is anything which lets you control the actions of other people. And office politics is the set of social relationships which you use to achieve this.

Power, of course, is what lets you achieve your goals – which is why it has been so important throughout history.

Many people tend to assume that office politics is just a layer of discussion on top of the 'important' stuff, the self-evident facts. This is not the case, politics gives meaning to the facts and helps you decide what the correct action to take will be. Politics doesn't provide you with a moral compass or require that you act with good intentions. Similarly there is a difference between 'moral' actions and 'effective' actions – sometimes these may be the same, sometimes they are not. In fact we'll see in this book that many actions you can take to improve your career are gleefully amoral.

At this point many people ask, quite reasonably, why they should be learning any of this. Surely it's enough to do an excellent job at your given tasks, impress your colleagues with this, and then ride that approval to a highly-placed and well-paying job? Right?

Well, no. The world is not fair, and the world of business even less so. Simply sitting there pretending that everything will be ok is a great way to find yourself left behind by those who *are* willing to play the game. If you want to excel in your career, then you will have to learn.

Still not convinced? Here are several good reasons to learn:

- **'Matrix'-style management is everywhere**: The traditional hierarchical organisation is fading away, being replaced by flat structures and 'matrix' management roles. You will find yourself leading a team of people who have no formal requirement to do what you say, and success will require you to lead them without having authority to back you up. This is only possible with persuasion and charm – the basic building blocks of office politics.
- **Jobs are changing faster than ever**: The days when we stayed in one company for our entire career are long gone. Short hops between roles create the fastest route up the organisational chart, which means you need to make a good impression fast. Understanding negotiation and influence lets you succeed even when you are new to the political power structure.
- **It works**: Simple as that, really.

First, however, you need to look at yourself and decide if you are really ready to engage in office politics. Hopefully the answer is 'yes' (else this will be a very short book), but there are several basic things which you need to internalise first.

- **Accept the idea of office politics**: One of the first things you need to do is to accept that office politics is not 'bad', or sleazy, or any of those terms which people throw around. Politics is a natural part of any group of people – it underlies our ability to lead others and to get things done, even in situations where the normal approach won't work. A team leader who understands politics is an incredible asset, one who can deliver success in the worst conditions.
- **Politics increases as you move up**: The higher you move in the company, the more your day-to-day work will involve political dealing and manoeuvring. But this is not to say that it is only useful for senior managers. Recognition and reward often come to the well-connected, and if this isn't you, then someone else will get the credit.
- **Commitment is vital**: You'll never achieve anything if you aren't able to commit. Life is hard, people will get in your way, random chance will pop up when you least expect it and ruin all of your plans. You'll want to give up, to just accept your current role 'for the moment' and take the low-risk approach. And you have to

ignore that feeling, and push yourself to keep going, even though it may seem impossible. This doesn't mean you ram your head against a brick wall until it falls over. Figure out your goals, aim for them, but be flexible in how you achieve them and even in how they appear in the end.

- **Embrace conflict**: You want to succeed, and so does everyone else. Win-win situations are a wonderful thing, albeit quite rare in reality. Conflict is a natural part of office politics, as we try to achieve our goals over the head of all the others trying to achieve theirs. If you don't have the stomach for conflict, then you aren't going to get very far. This doesn't mean that your whole career will be one eye-gouging bloodbath after another (probably, at least). But there will be conflict. And if you are known as someone who is willing to engage in a conflict, then you automatically make others think twice before they cross you. This makes your life easier (less eye-gouging required) and gives you a slightly clearer run at your goals.

- **Learn to compromise**: You can't fight with people all the time – no matter how successful, arseholes will eventually be dragged down by the hatred of their colleagues. Which means that you also need to build alliances, create networks of friends and respected co-workers. This requires compromises – sometimes you will need to set aside one of your goals to help others achieve theirs. You will need to modify our behaviour to suit the occasion, and recognise that bull-headed insistence is not always the best approach.

- **Take responsibility**: Stop thinking of yourself as the victim. Yes, life is tough, no, it's not easy to succeed. If it was easy, everyone would do it. Stop feeling desperate, feeling that your situation is out of control and the world is conspiring against you. Sure, the economy or your boss may suck, the politics of your current job may be stacked against you. But complaining doesn't help anything. Suck it up, see the world as one which you can change. You are responsible for your own success, all those problems are just challenges to crush and then boast about in your memoirs. Look at the problems, solve them, and learn for the future.

Office politics has limits, of course, just as any career-boosting technique does. The often-repeated quote about politics is that it is the "art of the *possible*", in that you probably won't achieve your perfect goal but you may still get the next-best thing.

Unfortunately for you, even though office politics is ubiquitous, most people are not really all that good at it. This seems like an odd thing to say – surely people who are bad at politics are the perfect company, as you can simply run through their plans to the management suite. In a way this is true – it is far easier to out-plot people who aren't plotting at all. But at the same time, those with limited skills make moves that the experienced would never even think of – random, chaotic approaches that give you no insight into their goals or motivations because they don't seem to match up with *anything*.

Office politics can be thought of as a way to get yourself closer to your goals. It usually won't be perfect. You will run into someone far better at scheming, or far more arbitrary with their decisions, or even just some insane management decision that will derail your carefully-designed plans. You need to be constantly adapting to the current situation and the potential wins you can have.

At the same time, you need to recognise the limits of your ability to influence others. Almost no-one is capable of consistently making decisions which are against their own interests. Some people do manage for a while (the noble ideal of self-sacrifice) or may simply not understand that a particular choice is less than ideal (an all-to-common problem). But you should *never* base any long term planning on this. Even the best idealist or the greatest fool will eventually realise that they can make other choices to improve their lives.

But if you accept and understand the limitations of power and influence, then there is certainly enough left over to boost your career far beyond your expectations.

2. Power in the workplace

The organisation around you is full of plans, programs, work-streams, efficiency drives, cost-cutting measures, and re-organisations. Any of these, perhaps even all of these, can have a major impact on your work, your job, or your career. In order to avoid the dangers and maximise the benefits to yourself, you need to be able to influence the events as they occur.

This ability to influence and control the happenings around you is the core principle of *power*. This is a nebulous factor, difficult to pin down or measure, yet extremely important when it comes to achieving anything of importance. Power can come from many different sources, although the most typical ones to be found within an organisation are as follows:

- Your position
- Your influence
- Your connections to other sources of power
- Your position as an expert
- Your control of a scarce resource

These sources are a mixture of formal and informal power, and we will cover all of them in the following sections.

What is formal and informal power?

There are many different ways in which we can influence the organisation around us. A number of them are *indirect* approaches to influence, working by creating a suitably receptive mindset in others and hoping that they will then accept your requests. This can be done in many ways, whether it be creating good impressions in onlookers, convincing your manager that you are their star employee, or getting the maximum loyalty and performance from your team.

The other approach to influencing others is *direct*, using your power within the workplace to 'strongly encourage' or even compel them to do what you want. Using direct power is a fast way to achieve results but can backfire badly if you push too hard. By contrast, indirect influence makes people *want* to help you, because they feel that some of your talent and competence will rub off on them.

As a general rule, a direct use of power will be built upon formal sources. The most common of these comes from the office which you hold and the formal organisational influence which you wield. Your position is a type of formal power – you are explicitly given permission by the company to tell people under you what to do and can seriously affect the outcome of their careers. This power is limited to your position, however – once you're out of the role, you can't influence events any further.

By contrast, indirect influence builds upon informal sources of power. These are not official, you cannot place them on an organisational chart and there is no reporting line between them, yet they exist because you have shown, somehow, that you deserve it.

One form of informal power is understanding how to work the bureaucracy. All large companies have some sort of official system in place to get things done. Those people who know how to use this system, or how to subvert it, have a level of power within the company – they are the ones you turn to when you have a difficult problem and the ones who you will want to have on your side when you need things done. Interestingly the most powerful people in an organisation may not be upper management– the old-timers who know all the processes are the ones who wield significant power behind the scenes.

This is also the case for any level of informal influence. The rank which a person holds within the company does not perfectly reflect their level of power. Figurehead bosses definitely exist – those who are on paper quite important but who really only exist to look good. The opposite type of boss also exists, the one with an unassuming title but a surprising amount of influence reaching throughout the company.

Sources of power
Your position
The most obvious source of power comes from your position within the organisation. If you are a manager, it is assumed that you will guide and focus the efforts of your team onto certain targets. If you are *good* manager, you will do this by working with your team member's strengths and interests. If you are a bad one, you will simply tell them what to do. In either case your position in the hierarchy lets you tell your direct reports what to do.

As you move higher in the organisation, your ability to directly control outcomes becomes less and less. Instead, you need to work through others – team leaders under you, etc. – in order to achieve anything. As a trade-off, your *overall* power increases as you are now able to direct many more activities – even if you no longer direct them as accurately as before. You will also find that higher positions have more power over decisions which are outside your group. This is partly because others want your input and agreement for cross-functional projects, but mostly because they are scared that you can screw over their career with your network.

This is not to say that non-managers derive no power from their position. Matrix leaders, experts in an area, or those who bring a lot of money into the company can have a large amount of influence indeed. But to grow beyond a certain level, you will need the additional power that subordinates can provide.

Your influence

Influence is one of the most common forms of informal power in society today, and it underlies the careers of a startling number of people. At the same time, 'influence' is a vague and nebulous thing, difficult to define or measure. So where does it come from?

The classical definition involves six main factors which will control the level of influence - and thus the amount of 'soft power' which you are able to exert in a situation. These are reciprocity, consistency, social proof, liking, authority, and scarcity. Clever use of these factors will allow you to influence others quite consistently, which in turn creates a base of power for use in office politics (and vice versa)

Reciprocity

Reciprocity is the need we have to pay others back for things they do for us. Essentially, we want to return a favour. This is excellent for building influence, because you can easily build up a sense of obligation in others by doing them favours – even if they didn't ask for it in the first place. Helping someone else builds this obligation, helping beyond what they would normally expect will build it even faster.

Consistency

We find it important to be consistent with actions we have previously taken or stances we have previously held. This can be easily abused to influence others. First ask for a small, almost insignificant initial commitment which is in line with your final goal. Most people will say yes, particularly if your request takes very little effort on their behalf. A week or so later, make a much larger request that builds upon that initial one. Because we like to be internally consistent, it is very difficult for people to completely reject such a request when they have already accepted the smaller one.

Social proof
We take the actions of others as a guide for our own actions. Think of trends, viral marketing, the way people line up behind others even if there is nothing at the head of the line. By pointing out the actions others have taken, particularly when they line up with your current request, you prime others to believe that this is a standard and thus highly reasonable thing to be doing.

Liking
Everyone is more helpful to, and more influenced by, those they like. Fortunately for influencers everywhere, 'liking' is based on a fairly simple set of rules. We like people who are like us. We like people who compliment us (even if it's not all the sincere). And we like people who share mutual goals with us.

Authority
People value the opinion of those who they feel are knowledgeable experts. This is most apparent when this expertise relates to the subject at hand (which you would hope to see, after all), but it also leaks over into other fields – hence the value we place on doctor's opinions, even in completely unrelated areas. Thus your influence in an area can be improved by highlighting your qualifications, or (better yet) *getting someone else* to highlight it for you. This provides authority and social proof in one go – a double bonus.

Scarcity
We all want what we cannot have – and when we finally get it, we want to show it off. This is the core principle behind luxury goods and it also works for influence building. By making something rare and difficult to obtain, you turn it into something valuable. You can use this effect to artificially limit membership in a group or even access to yourself, thereby making it more sought-after.

Your connections to other sources of power
Everyone in the organisation has some sort of power inherent in their role and their relationships with others. In many cases this is an insignificant amount and they are regularly pushed around at the whim of others in the company. If you want to get past this point, to develop your career and

influence beyond that of the average peon, then you need to increase the level of power you can access. And one of the simplest ways to do this is to connect with other sources of power.

Exchanges and competition for power tends to work in two different directions, depending on who you are dealing with. You can think of these as the vertical and horizontal relationships.

In the horizontal, you are dealing with people who are your peers or near-peers. As you generally spend a lot of time with people at this level, you will find that alliances and cartels tend to naturally build amongst the members. These can be powerful in much the same way as a union can be powerful – it provides an aligned opinion on a subject which is made stronger by repetition through all the voices. Unfortunately, the horizontal dimension is also one in which you are dealing with your competition. To be blunt, these people are the ones you need to beat – the ones you must outwit and outplay in order to receive the next promotion, the high-profile project, or the new job.

In the vertical, you are dealing with those who either have more or less power than you. As you would expect, gaining the interest of those with more power is vital for your own rise in the career. But just as important, (and often overlooked) is gaining the support of those with *less* power. Politics is very often an exchange between someone who wants to *gain* power and a group of people who want to *give them* that power, because the group believes that the one person will promote their interests. If you can successfully convince a group of people that you are best able to represent them, then you are already on your way up the corporate ladder.

Your position as an expert

Being known as an 'expert' provides you a level of power in the organisation – your opinion is valued more than others, which means you are in turn able to exert greater influence on business decisions. The power you can exert in this way is proportional to the apparent value of your expertise – the more important it is to the core business or success of the company, the more important you are.

Gaining this position is surprisingly easy – simply doing your job better than anyone else in the company will instantly make you an expert of sorts. On-the-job experience, in which you naturally come into contact with the different facets of your role, will build this expertise and thus the perception of your value. Deliberately going in-depth within your subject to become a true expert, particularly if you can get some form of professional qualification, will make you truly valued.

There are limitations to this approach. The power you exert is often limited to areas directly impacting your area of expertise – you will find yourself pigeonholed unless you actively try to branch out into new areas. Similarly, you are only valued if your area of expertise is relevant. Being an expert in the old processes is useless if the entire organisation is doing something completely different.

For these reasons it is rarely worth planning your long-term political campaigns on the basis of power as an expert. Use it as an initial starting point, yes, use it to gain access to higher levels of management during discussions, but it is only valuable in the long run if you are able to stay up-to-date with changing fashions.

Your control of a scarce resource

In office politics, as in the wider world, having control over a scarce resource provides you with a source of power and influence. This only applies if the resource is actually valued, of course, but provided you are able to find the right resource then you will find your opinion is suddenly much more valued.

Unlike the economic world (where resources such as coal and lumber are important), office politics uses a set of resources which many may not even recognise as being important. Some of the most relevant ones include:

- **Funding**: Money makes the world go round – it provides salaries, funding for projects, the ability to increase headcount, etc. etc. If you control a source of available funding, particularly during a period when the company is trying to reduce spending, then you are able to heavily influence the decisions which are being made.
- **Access**: Access to powerful people or politically important projects is also a scarce resource, as these are not open to everyone. Providing this access in exchange for favours is a long-established method of creating a power base – the power which administrative assistants wield is a simple example of this. Note that it is a 'borrowed' source of power, in that your influence lasts only as long as the person you are gatekeeping for is considered important.

- **Favours**: People with larger networks tend to collect a lot of favours from others over the years. After enough time, the favour network can be wide enough to achieve truly startling things – but only if they decide to help. The rarity of an all-encompassing collection of favours makes the owner a political force to be accounted for.
- **Technology**: Technology brings efficiency, speed, and savings, while requiring significant budgets to implement across the organisation. Both of these make the people in charge of new tech important, particularly if it is a 'hot' area or one where business leaders really want it implemented *now*.
- **Expertise**: As described in the previous section, knowledge or expertise in an area is also a resource. If you are the only one who has the necessary degree of knowledge in the field, then you are now controlling a scare resource, with the corresponding importance that this implies.

Using power, sensibly

Once you have power, or at least realise that you have power, then the temptation to use it is often overwhelming. Temptation often occurs when a big event is coming up – particularly one where you stand to lose or gain a lot. This is exactly the point where you need to be careful, not only are you new to the world of political power, but other people will also be trying to influence the outcome (and usually doing it better than you). Newcomers invariably push too far, too fast, and end up making a huge mess of things. To avoid this, you need to be objective and realistic about your situation. Only by looking clearly at what is occurring around you will it be possible to plan your campaign of influence.

This, of course, requires you to develop a certain level of situational awareness – an essential skill for anyone aiming to climb the corporate ladder. Given how valuable it is in reading the underlying currents of a group, you may as well start as soon as you can, even if you are relatively powerless in your position.

The first step is to create a *non-political* summary of the situation, one in which only the logical consequences of the situation are taken into consideration. Then ask yourself what the next actions would be if everyone were a robot, devoid of emotion and only interested in the best outcome for themselves. Although this is unrealistic, it at least gives you an idea of how things are likely to go – very few people can consistently act against their own interests all the time.

Once this is in place, you need to examine the far more complex world of influence, values, and desires. This is hugely challenging, as you will need to make a number of guesses about other people and will have no way of knowing if they are accurate or not. Nonetheless, it is worth doing and will give you a far better idea of the outcomes. Few things are as satisfying as watching a complicated situation unfold as you expected it to.

The overview of the situation which you develop should include several distinct pieces of information:

- **People involved**: Who are the people involved in the situation? What are their roles, both official and unofficial? What are their goals or preferred outcomes, and what are their expectations? This last question is often difficult to answer, as you rarely have all information on the people involved – you will need to use your judgement to compile a 'most-likely' position.
- **Values involved**: Everyone has a different set of internal values, derived from their cultural background, attitudes and beliefs. It can be dangerous to base your calculations of peoples actions based on broad stereotypes, but often an insight into the belief of the actors in any situation can help you predict what their intentions will be.
- **Spheres of influence**: As we've previously mentioned, everyone has a sphere of influence inside which they can change the outcome of events. This may be due to explicit power (lines of reporting, etc.) or 'soft' power. You should have a reasonable estimate of the sphere of influence for each major player in the situation. You should also have an idea of what they *believe* their influence to be – an entirely different matter to what is actually the case!
- **Strengths & weaknesses**: In close-fought situations even minor differences in relative skills can mean vast changes in the final outcome. You should understand the main strengths and weaknesses of all players in the situation – including yourself…

At this point you should a reasonable idea of who is involved in the big event. The next question is whether you should be involved as well. Remember that there are always political tussles going on, but getting involved in all of them will burn you out and turn everyone against you. Ask yourself several questions:

- **Does the situation allow me to intervene?** Are things in a suitably flexible state in which it is possible to push things in one particular direction? Or is the change coming like a freight train, impossible to redirect without sacrificing your career?
- **Can I achieve anything?** Do you have the level of influence or power which would be required to make changes to the situation? Do the other people involved have a high enough opinion of you that you could achieve something? Would they listen to you?
- **Am I competitive?** Are your strengths and weaknesses sufficient in comparison to the other people involved? Will they help you to carry your interests through in case of pressure or pushback from the others? Are you, to put it simply, good enough?

The answers to these questions will give you an idea of where you need to exert your effort in order to achieve something. The next steps you take, much like the next section to read in this book, are dependent on your situation.

If you cannot understand your **position in the event**, such as where you stand, what power you exert, and how you would do so, then you need to work on situational awareness. Look at Chapter 4 (page 33) to learn about understanding your situation and self.

If you are simply **not competitive**, in that your political power or influence is not sufficient to do *anything*, then you should pull out of the competition. Let others fight, go back and spend time building up your reputation amongst the company so that you have a better chance in the next round. See Chapters 5, 6 and 7 on developing your reputation within the company.

If your power base is sufficient, but **no-one listens to you**, then your office politics skills are lacking. Start with the fundamentals in Chapter 8 (page 92) and move on from there.

If you are in a situation where you can only act via **direct reporting lines**, then you need to ensure that your manager and team are fully on board with what you are doing. Look into Chapter 9 (page 119) and Chapter 10 (page 129) for information on dealing with these.

If you need assistance from a broader set of people, but **do not have a network**, then it is time to start building one (the ideal time was a few years ago, but starting now is better than starting tomorrow). Turn to Chapter 11 (page 145).

If you have the right connections, are moderately persuasive, but **not persuasive enough** to get what you need, then it is time to work on your influence and negotiation skills. See Chapter 12 and 13, (pages 155 and 171) for details of these skills.

If you are persuasive, well-connected, but still **about to lose badly** in this exchange, then it is time to think about risk minimisation or (in the worst case) finding a new job. Check out Chapters 14 and 15 (page 194 and 200) for more information on this.

3. Political skills to develop

What makes a successful politician or successful leader? As with all things in life, politics is a skill, something which you can improve with practice.

More precisely, it is an umbrella term for a number of different skills, each of which can be used to help your career. These skills are built to varying degrees upon four main components – namely observation, implementation, networking, and apparent sincerity. You will need to build up your skill in each of these if you want to truly shine in the world of office politics.

- **Observation**: Office politics requires reading and interpreting the signals given off by people around you – what they want, where they are going, how they are doing it. If you cannot understand others, you cannot plan to influence them. If you cannot understand your organisation, you cannot determine the best way to act. And if you cannot understand yourself... then what exactly are you doing?
- **Implementation**: Once you've made a plan, you need to implement it. Knowing the right people to approach, the right tactics to use, the right timing, the right attitude – all of these are vital parts of getting the plan out of your head and into the real world.
- **Networking**: The relationships you build within and beyond your organisation are the ones you use to gather information, discover opportunities, and progress your agenda.
- **Apparent sincerity**: Everyone prefers to deal with those who are sincere, we instinctively distrust those who seem dishonest or tricky. Your success is based on other believing that you are sincere in your actions. This doesn't mean you actually *are* sincere, merely that you *appear* to be so.

Seems easy enough, doesn't it? These components are combined to make the various skills required for office politics, as discussed in the following sections. Later chapters in this book will show how they can be developed and utilised.

Acting

Acting is a fundamental skill in the world of office politics. Being able to hide your true feelings and persuade others using somewhat-less-than-perfect-truthfulness is vital to achieving your goals. One of the first steps towards becoming a skilled political animal is accepting that you are going to deliberately lie to people, and that *this is ok*. Consciously acknowledging that you will be acting is the cornerstone of doing it well.

This doesn't mean you will always be playing a role. Indeed, the closer you can make your work persona and your actual personality, the easier it will be. But acting should be used whenever you have a specific target which needs to be persuaded. Moving up the chain of management requires you to get better and better at acting, to the point that higher levels are constantly evaluating their own and others personae.

Acting is like any other skill – the more you practice it, the better you will be. If you are happy with your current role and ability then there is no real problem, but being able to act will improve your career chances immensely. You can take several steps which may help your skills in this area:

- If you have a specific conversation coming up, then imagine how this will play out in advance. Act it out in front of a mirror, observing your body language and speech. You may feel a bit ridiculous, but holding a conversation in your head is simply no substitute for *seeing and hearing* how it looks.
- If you have a goal where serious acting ability is required, then you may need to be serious about developing the skill. One of the cheapest, if time-consuming, ways to do this is to join an amateur theatre group. These will give you training in general acting skills and, as a bonus, have ridiculously complex internal politics going on to practice with.
- Look at your work environment and determine where you can fit in. Can you deliberately cast yourself as an expert in a field, thus enhancing your reputation and giving you more independence? Can you alter your work persona to better fit the company culture, or (better yet) your manager's image of an ideal employee? Start with small steps, then work your way up to large changes

Mimicry

Mimicry is the art of mirroring actions, mannerisms and words of those you are speaking to. It is a highly useful technique when dealing with others, as it creates a level of connection between you and the person you are mimicking. If you've ever felt that a salesman seems to just connect with

Political skills to develop

you, coincidentally leading to you spending a lot of money, then you've probably experienced this.

Almost everyone engages in mimicry to some extent – after all, we adopt the same speech patterns as our friends and usually dress in the same way. But some people are much better at it than others, deliberately analysing the company they are in and consciously adjusting their behaviour to better fit in. They remember typical phrases that the others used, sneaking them into their own sentences at the right time. They choose clothes which match the styles of their targets. And they adopt similar mannerisms to those they meet.

Although we do not all need to become perfect mimics, empty of our own personality, a certain level of skill is vital to your career. Progression requires that your manager and colleagues actually like you, and this is made easier if they think you are 'one of them'. It doesn't have to be much, but the occasional spot of mimicry is both effective and very difficult for others to spot.

The counterpoint to this is that mimicry should not be so obvious that it can be spotted. Don't just copy everything they do, this is very obvious to even the least-observant. If other people realise that you are deliberately trying to force a feeling of rapport, the immediate loss of trust is very difficult to regain.

Mimicking external patterns

There are a number of external cues which we give off when interacting, and each of these can be (carefully) mimicked to increase rapport:

- **Posture**: Body posture is an external cue written in large print – it is easy to see and easy to match. Look at your counterpart and their body language – are they sitting straight, slouching to the side, crossing their legs, holding something (inevitably a pen or cup of coffee)? Watch as they change position, wait about 5 seconds, and then follow suit. Take care to match their speed – move faster or slower until you're moving at roughly the same rate.
- **Gestures**: Gestures are an important part of communication, giving emphasis and subtext to the words we speak. Matching gestures is more challenging to do well – try to observe each one separately and in context. Are some gestures consistently performed? Hands only or is the head involved as well? Expansive

or restrictive? Watch and then try to *discreetly* mirror these – always wait a few seconds first, and don't make it obvious.
- **Facial expressions**: Facial expressions are highly mobile and very difficult to match. You will need to look at multiple different possible expressions to identify those which could be matched, and matching them without appearing to be mocking is challenging at best.

Mimicking language and voice

External actions are all very well, but language is based on words and the way we say them. Being able to mimic your counterparts' language and voice is difficult, but highly effective.

- **Tone**: Matching your counterparts' tone is something that needs to be indirect and subtle. You (obviously) cannot raise your voice several octaves to match theirs, but you can subtly shift your pitch up or down slightly in their direction. Subtly drift towards your counterpart, but stay natural.
- **Speed**: Everyone has a natural pace when speaking, be it rapid and clipped or slow and chilled. A complete mismatch in pace will lead to a break in rapport, your counterpart will think that you are either too damn fast or too damn slow. Subtly shading your pace towards theirs is a good way to make a 'natural' connection without talking like a caricature.
- **Word choice**: This one is slightly more complicated, as it involves the way we prefer to observe the world. Most people will tend to favour one of the four modes of sensing – seeing, hearing, feeling, and thinking. They will use phrases which are based on this favoured mode, and will respond better to you when your conversation follows this mode as well. Deliberately shifting your conversation to include some of these typical phrases (as shown below) will make them feel comfortable with you and your discussion.
    - **Seeing**: Uses phrases focused on terms such as looking, clarity, focusing, 'picturing things', and brightness
    - **Hearing**: Phrases revolve around sound, listening, music, 'tuning in' and the like.
    - **Feeling**: Will discuss experiences based on touching, feeling, whether something is fuzzy or hard, as well as using phrases such as 'getting in touch'.

- o **Thinking**: Moves beyond sensing and into understanding, as they use phrases such as learning, deciding, considering, experiencing, and knowing.

Mimicry made simple: copy the last few words

People like those who are similar to them, almost at an unconscious level. There are a number of overly-complicated approaches to fake similarity, usually grouped under the term 'mirroring', which involve matching body language, tones, stances, all sorts of things. Generally this is too much effort for most people, so it's worth focusing on a simpler process: mirror the last couple of words they said.

How does this work in practice? Listen to the last thing they have said. If you want further information, or need to build rapport, then simply repeat the last couple of words from their sentence. Add a slight upwards inflection to your voice to make it an implied question. You should give the impression that you need their help to understand. They will inevitably expand on their previous statement, giving you more information.

This is simple and, importantly, fairly subtle if done well. Do not try to over-enthusiastically mirror every sentence and match every motion or posture they do – this is more obvious than you think and will irritate your counterpart immensely.

Flattery

Flattery is the act of making others feel better than they really are – you can also think of it as strategically praising them to achieve a goal. The goal can be big or small, long term or short, but flattery will help you reach it in one way or another. It is a very popular technique in office politics, because it works. There are very few people who are able to completely ignore another person giving them praise, and even those that do seem immune will be swayed if the flattery is cleverly done.

Note the last part here – flattery is *only* successful if it is undetected by your target. Once they have realised that you are doing this, every single interaction you have in the future will be considered to be false in some way. Deliberate flattery needs to be subtle, targeted, and used rarely.

So how do you achieve this? Here are a few tips:

- **Stay as close as possible to the truth**: If you actually admire or appreciate something about the other person, use this as your basis

– it will make the entire conversation sound far more believable. If they do something well or beyond the usual requirements, congratulate them. Give credit to others where it is due, as this allows you to flatter them without a second thought.

- **Be specific**: A highly-specific compliment appears far more real than a generalised 'you did a great job on that project'. Put some thought into what you say. This is also a valuable defence against flatterers – ask them what *precisely* they liked about your previous work.
- **Try to be different**: Aim to compliment something which they have not heard from many other people beforehand. It takes more research, but will help you stand out from the crowd as a 'natural' compliment.
- **Ask for advice**: Particularly if it is on a topic they consider themselves to be an expert on. This feeds their ego while allowing you to subtly praise their level of knowledge in the field. Note that they do not need to be an actual expert in the field, merely that they believe themselves to be one.
- **Target specific attributes**: If you do need to flatter someone where it is not deserved, pick an attribute which they are proud of or one which you are considered well-placed to compliment. This ensures that they are unlikely to notice or reject your praise, which gives you more room to work with.
- **Don't overdo it**: Constant flattery is obvious to all but the most self-absorbed. Be subtle, provide a small amount of flattery on rare occasions. This makes it seem like a true compliment and gives you the image of honesty.

Trading favours

Everyone likes getting things for free – even more so when it comes in the form of help at work. Doing additional work or favours for others in the organisation is an easy way to increase their opinion of you. Even more helpfully, even a favour given 'for free', with no request for payback, will still create a feeling of reciprocity in your counterpart. This makes favour-giving a simple way to build up a network of people who you can call on for help at a later stage.

It is important to consider favours strategically – you should not be acting as the trashcan for all jobs which no-one wants to do. If you are being treated in this way, stop it. No-one respects (or promotes) those who cannot say 'no' to useless tasks. Instead ensure that any favour you grant is somehow in line with your goals, whether it be via impressing someone whose help you need, sneaking into a group of more-important colleagues, or even as a long-term plan to replace another.

Some more detail on that last point – favours can also be used as a way to displace others from roles or responsibilities which you would like. Any role has tasks which are less appealing, yet crucial to overall success. Offer to take these on, be friendly and helpful. If necessary, offer to do even more irrelevant and menial tasks to gain trust. Use this as a stepping stone to help with more important tasks, being careful to tell the relevant manager that you are involved. There will inevitably be a point where the main responsible cannot do the job, usually as they are away on holidays – this is your moment to step in and do an exceptional job, one which is obviously better than the one you are replacing. The quality of your output, combined with careful praising of your own work, is the start of gaining this role permanently.

If you are looking to use favour-trading in a typical, non-malicious way, then there are a few things to keep in mind:

- **Be broad in your helpfulness**: Much like your personal network, you should aim to have a wide range of people who are in your debt (either explicitly or implicitly). This gives you the best chance of calling in useful help when needed. Be careful to maintain and renew these contacts every so often, lest they forget about you and your help. See our later section on networking (page 145) for some more tips.
- **Never ask right away**: Asking for a favour directly after providing one makes it very clear that you are trading support, and this tends to make people feel uncomfortable. They will likely help you this time, but not a second. Leave a delay to build up more credibility before calling favours in.
- **Be strategic and specific**: Favours are a currency, and this currency can be used up. Call in favours for important topics, ones where you need that persons help to achieve something which relates to your goals. When you do ask them, be specific in what you require so that they can understand what to do – remember

that a solution to the problem may be clear to you, but a mystery to others.
- **Target your favours to their needs**: All of us have different needs and wants in an organisation, which translates into different 'currencies' which we are looking to trade. Try to match what you are offering with what they need to maximise the value of any favour you provide. Some more information on this is provided in a later section (page 159).

Assertiveness

Assertiveness is all about promoting your point of view in the face of other people's disagreement. Making demands, setting deadlines for others, following up on work done, picking apart excuses – assertiveness is a requirement for getting your own way in the office. This doesn't mean you are angry or argumentative, you can be as calm and friendly as you like. But you are firm on what you want and you are willing to ignore others to get it.

There is a time and a place for assertiveness, and one of the most dangerous places to try it is when discussing with your managers. For all that management talks about wanting self-confident employees who will challenge authority, this rarely extends to wanting people who say 'no' to their requests. By all means point out when an idea is unwise or unlikely to achieve their goals, but if it truly comes down to a direct order, being assertive is likely to get you fired.

Developing your assertiveness is a long and complex process, but the beginning points are as follows:

- **Value yourself**: You are competent and destined to go far, you bring value to your organisation and to others around you. Understanding this is the root of self-confidence, self-confidence is an essential aspect of assertiveness. Just don't go overboard into being an arsehole.
- **State your desires**: You (presumably) know what your needs and wants are, so ensure that your discussions make this clear. It's very easy to assume that others will 'just understand' what you need – this is unfortunately almost never the case. If you want something, say it.

Political skills to develop

- **...Confidently**: Be confident in talking about what you want. Don't be scared off by the reactions of others, push through and keep focusing on that topic. Is it scary? Yes. But every time you consciously keep the focus on your own needs, you get a bit better at being assertive.
- **Stop apologising**: It's easy to get into the habit of apologising when you have done nothing wrong, in an attempt to make others feel better about a minor disagreement. This will weaken your resolve and subconsciously deflect you from asserting your will. So stop it.
- **Learn to say no**: Saying no is one of the most important things you can do, it will save you vast amounts of trouble over the years. Practice saying no to small requests, then work your way up to bigger ones. You will likely feel uncomfortable afterwards, which is ok – this is the feeling we want to get used to.

Self-promotion

Occasionally you will get lucky and have a manager who is fully invested in discovering and promoting your competence to others in the organisation. I have yet to see it happen, but it is theoretically possible. For the majority of us, it is important to *self-promote* – to put the effort into appearing competent and showing our colleagues that we are competent. After all, if you don't do it, who will?

Self-promotion is difficult to do well, appearing boastful and vain if overdone. Not doing it at all is just as bad, as your achievements go overlooked by those around you. But when done well, self-promotion is an excellent way to get yourself noticed, subtly remind others of your contributions, and place yourself in a stronger position for pay negotiations.

So how do you do it well?

- **Match your activity to the culture**: If the organisation is highly political, promote yourself at every chance you get. If it's all about a greater cause than the employees, then do it subtly and carefully. If it is an organisation with a strong sense of teamwork, then focus your claims on your benefit to the team.
- **Understand your limits**: Successful self-promotion requires an understanding of both what you have achieved and your network within the company. Those who have no connection to you are

unlikely to care about your successes, so why waste your time telling them? Focus on those who will care and who will take this into salary or promotion-related meetings.

Networking

Networking is the art of making connections across and outside the organisation, specifically connections that are useful to you in your job or career. It's important to remember that this is not about your immediate colleagues and managers, a healthy network needs to spread widely amongst people who are not necessarily useful now, but may be in the future. Successful careers tend to build upon a strong network, because this breadth of connections brings you more options.

As part of understanding yourself and your career, you should have determined roughly where you want to be in the future (or at least have several different scenarios which seem reasonable). The political skill involved in networking lies in understanding who may be useful to help reach future roles, and who might be better avoided (or in extreme cases, removed). You will often find that like-minded people develop groups dedicated to promoting all of their interests – this is known as coalition-building and is common everywhere a large number of people are working together. Try to identify the coalitions which exist within your department and organisation, and see if you can work your way onto them. Much like the 'old school tie' networks, entering a large coalition can give you significant benefits.

Doing this, of course, requires that you put the effort in to be sociable and get along with others. Some people hate this, others love it. If you want to succeed in your career, you should try to master this skill as well. Some basic tips are below, however we have devoted an entire chapter to building and maintaining a network below (page 145).

- **Plan it out**: Like any goal, a strong network needs to be worked towards. Make a list of people you know and a list of people you would like to know. Using those lists, create a plan covering how you will make initial connections (for those you don't know) or strengthen the existing connections (for those you do). Update this plan as time goes on – you will find that the needs of your network changes over time.
- **Focus efforts before going wide**: If you are trying to expand into a new network, it is far more effective to focus your charm

offensive on one to two key members *before* connecting with the rest of the group. The goodwill you create with these initial contacts will help open doors to discussions with the others.
- **Target overlapping networks**: If you always talk to the same people, you will soon find that the circle of possible acquaintances reaches a natural limit – everyone will know everyone in a small enough group. At this point you will need to look into similar but not *directly* related networks and try to enter these – you will often find one or two people overlap, which lets you expand into new groups.
- **Help people**: Your network is a two-way street, and you should always be trying to help those who you are in contact with. Nothing creates a stronger sense of connection (and reciprocity) than offering someone help with their issues.
- **Connect those in your network**: In line with the point above, always try to connect someone from your network to someone else who may be able to help them. This of course requires you to know the challenges and strengths of those in your network, but it allows you to deliver useful help to those who need it.

Actively building a reputation

Your reputation is the sum of the beliefs that others hold about you, both positive and negative. It comes from direct interactions (when you work with or talk to others) and from indirect gossip by others about you. In general, the further someone is from your position (both in the hierarchy and in regardless to role) the more likely they are to know about you via secondary sources alone.

This means that building a strong reputation and building a strong network are closely linked together – a network of people who like you is far better at spreading the good word than an unaffiliated mass who don't really care.

A good reputation is important to have for many reasons. It strongly affects your chances to receive promotion, pay, and new offers. It gives you the aura of competence and value. And it encourages others to believe that your actions, however Machiavellian they may be, are completely trustworthy and altruistic. All of these lead to a stronger position in the organisation, which in turn allows you more opportunities to build your reputation.

Building a reputation is mostly a matter of achieving success and telling others about it, however there are a few factors which you can focus on which strongly improve your positive reputation:

- **Quality and rarity**: Achievements by themselves are fine, but achieving things which are both rare and unusual will provide a greater boost to your reputation. This can be as dramatic as summiting Everest or as mundane as attending a top-tier University – the important factor is that you have done something beyond that of normal people.
- **Networking**: Spreading a good reputation requires people who will talk well of you, and that is where a strong and wide network will pay off.
- **Style of working**: The way you work carries as much weight as what you achieve. Those who can achieve success while remaining cheerful, proactive, and in-control are considered to be more effective than the grizzled screamers of the world.

4. Understand your current situation

No amount of clever office politics will help you progress if you are incompetent or overwhelmed, and so your first step is to determine your current situation and how it could be improved.

The underlying skill needed here is that of perceptiveness, the ability to *see and understand* the many things which are going on around you in the workplace. The significant look, the forwarded email, the accidental failure to copy you on an important announcement. Do you notice when these occur? Do you understand what they mean? And more importantly, what you can do about it?

Perceptiveness is the basic skill upon which your entire approach to office politics hangs. If you cannot perceive and interpret actions and underlying thoughts, how will you be able to plan an appropriate response?

There are three main areas where you need to develop skills in perceptiveness:

- **Understanding others**: Understanding the thoughts or emotions of others around you as you speak to them, using this to estimate their intentions, and then modifying the way you act to achieve your goals.
- **Understanding yourself**: You need to know your own goals in order to achieve them. But you cannot stop there – an understanding of your own weaknesses, strengths, and emotional reaction to certain challenges will allow you to develop strategies around them.
- **Understanding the organisation**: The org chart looks pretty, but tells you nothing. You need to understand how the company works, who the important people are, who you need to impress or to network with or to discuss future jobs with.

Much like any other skill, perceptiveness develops through use. This section will provide some useful starting questions to help understand yourself and the organisation, the remainder of the book will cover understanding and influencing others. But despite the information we provide, in the end the most effective way to develop is to *try* – actively assess people and situations you encounter, try to determine the underlying interests at play, watch and understand the world around you. Hard? Yes, absolutely. But worthwhile.

Understanding yourself

There are all sorts of clever quotes about understanding yourself out there, we're not going to mention any of them here – it's too tacky. But understanding what you want and what matters most to you is very important for reaching your goals. Many people say something vague and hand-wavy like "I want to make a difference" or "I want a job that fulfils me". This is essentially useless, you need to *think* about what you want and determine it in detail.

Is this hard work? Yes, yes it is. You'll need to look at your talents, skills, and interests, and then put a lot of work into deciding which career will best suit them. You'll also need to discover how you are contributing to the problems in your life. Both of these are hard topics, both of these require a lot of effort. But you need to suck it up and figure it out.

Your core values

There are a couple of points which you should consider when determining your 'values' – the things which you truly find important and which thus most strongly affect your happiness in the job. They can be thought of as intangible, tangible, and lifestyle values.

Look at the examples given below, and decide which of these are most important to you (it's sometimes easiest to rank them from most to least important). Are there any overlaps? Do the values fit together? Can you spend some time thinking of the ways these values could fit into a job? Yes? Then use this as a basis for deciding on your next steps.

Tangible values are the rewards you get for coming to work, such as:

- **Impressive salaries**: Is money important to you? Do you want to earn more than others, even if it requires significantly more hours in the office?
- **Travelling for work**: The world is large, and many jobs include significant amounts of travel. Is this exciting, or would you rather have a steady home base and regular working environment?
- **Flexible hours**: Setting your hours can be key to finding a work-life balance, while others prefer the structure that the typical workday provides.
- **Vacation**: How many days would you like to have off per year? Is this more important than the salary?

Understand your current situation

- **Working autonomously**: Some prefer autonomous jobs with minimal oversight, others look to be part of a well-guided team.

Intangible values are those which keep us motivated and engaged, bringing us into work on those terrible Mondays when the coffee machine is broken. For example:

- **Variety and change**: Do you prefer a set routine, or do you want new things every day?
- **Helping others**: Do you want to work for a company with a good cause or charitable works?
- **Feeling respected**: Do you want a culture in which everyone is respected for their input, or one where only a few have that honour? (This usually assumes that you would be one of the few)
- **Risk-taking**: Are you risk averse, after a safe position? Or do you like the thrill of risky events and challenges?
- **Public recognition**: Are you happy with working on your project, or do you crave public recognition from higher management?

Lifestyle values are those which affect your free time, the life you have outside work. This may include:

- **Time with friends and family**: Do you want free evenings and weekends to spend with others? Or are you happy with long nights and overtime hours?
- **Big city living**: Do you need a big city, with a café on every corner and a bar across the street? Or would you rather the quieter life of the suburbs or countryside?
- **Living overseas**: Do you want to leave your hometown and native country to pursue your career? Or are you attached to home?
- **Saving up money**: Are you more interested in saving cash for later, or spending it on the good things now? High cost of living areas or low salaries can make it hard to do either.
- **A place of your own**: Want to buy a house or apartment? This depends on your salary and local costs – which in turn affects the jobs you might take. Or would you rather keep the flexibility of renting?

Once you have figured out these core values, you need to decide how they feed into your overall career goals and your specific requirements at the moment. Office politics is very much about knowing what you want to have and what is standing in the way of you getting it. It's the art of aiming for option #1, but still keeping option #2 in mind as a back-up plan in case everything falls apart.

This of course means that you need to be realistic with yourself. You have limited resources, both in political capital and time, which means you need to use them for maximum effectiveness. You need to recognise the conditions and constraints which would stop you from achieving your success, and you need to decide how you can overcome them. Or even *if* you can overcome them – sometimes you may have to give up on the perfect ideal and focus on more realistic goals. The important thing is to make sure that even these 'second-rate' goals should be in line with your core values

Are you an introvert or extrovert?
There are two basic groups which all people fall into, the introverts and extroverts. There are many different ways of classifying these two, but we will go with a fairly simple one: an extrovert takes decisions based on input from the outside world, an introvert based on input from within themselves.

Both introverts and extroverts tend to have different ways of thinking about the world, and thus tend to distrust one another – introverts believe that extroverts are flighty and easily swayed while extroverts believe that introverts are weird and need to get out more. Neither of them are better than the other, but it is important to understand which group you belong. This lets you understand your own goals and your own reactions to events.

If you can't decide this right now, then take some time to think about your life and your beliefs. Where do your personal laws or absolute beliefs come from? Are they formed more by society, as for extroverts, or more from personal conviction or rational decisions, as for introverts? Are you more comfortable in larger groups or in solitude? Do you prefer to fit into society or go your own way?

Your political style
The next question to ask is what your preferred political 'style' is. Your style (and the style of those you work with) is the underlying base upon which all of your political manoeuvring will be built.

- **Apolitical** people are completely uninterested in office politics, they believe that hard work and following set rules is enough to achieve success. They are very honest, trust others, and like to work

Understand your current situation

with those who feel the same way. Their lack of interest causes problems in highly-political organisations, and this limits their development inside the organisation.

- **Team players** believe success comes through the success of the group, and use political favours to advance the groups' needs ahead of their own. They are comfortable with limited political trading but prefer working according to set or informal rules to bring their team to success.
- **Individualists** are focused on their own goals rather than that of the group, and their efforts reflect this. They are happy to use either political trading or formal rules to get what they want. They enjoy the negotiations and intrigue of office politics, seeing it as a fun challenge to work around the system.
- **Political natives** also focus on their own goals, but believe that the best way to achieve them is by playing politics. They tend to be subtle, look for subtleties and ulterior motives in others, and have no difficulty in crushing opponents who stand in their way. They make terrible team players and gravitate towards highly-political organisations.

Your political skill

Each political style contains people with a certain level of political talent and ability. As discussed in the previous section, political skills tend to rely to a varying extent on four core components. As a rule of thumb, the better you are at all of these areas, the more likely you will succeed in your career – and better, skill in these areas can compensate for a lack of talent or hard-work.

Look at the core components which are described below, and try to honestly rate yourself regarding talent in these areas. You may be terrible in one or two (or even all) areas – this is ok. It is better to know now, and plan to build up your skills, than to falsely assume that you are an expert already.

Observation

This is the art of 'reading' others, the ability to see beyond what others are saying, looking at their body language and tones to determine what they are really trying to get across. It also includes a sense of self-awareness to understand what others think when they see you – and also how your behaviour affects them. Socially perceptive people are excellent at determining the hidden currents of office politics and spotting when others are lying to them.

Implementation

The ability to implement your plans by convincing others, essentially affecting how and what they think. Successfully influencing others requires a strong understanding of what their goals and preferences, which then moves into careful crafting of your message to create maximum appeal for them. Highly influential people make strong leaders, and tend to have no problems getting their projects moved forward even in tough times.

Networking

Networking is the ability to form wide-ranging relationships with many different people inside (and outside) the organisation. Keeping a large network running requires a surprising amount of effort, as each of these contacts needs to be revisited at a regular interval. Those with strong networks always know the best person to speak to, and are regularly able to solve problems via back-channel connections which the majority had never even heard of.

Apparent sincerity

The ability to *appear* to be honest and open. This does not relate to how honest you *actually* are, as onlookers cannot judge if you are an angel or a demon. But they can make a judgement on how you appear to be, and this is where the ability to seem sincere is important. Those who appear sincere gain a reputation of honesty, and others are more likely to trust their plans and judgement. In other words, it is not important to *be* sincere, it is important to *seem* sincere.

How are you perceived by others?

It's perfectly fine to work out what *you* want, your core values and overall desires. But this book focuses on achieving your goals through interactions with others, which means you need to understand how you are perceived by *others*. In fact, you will often find that it is completely different to your self-image.

Before you go into details, ask yourself a few questions regarding your current situation. Your goal here is to decide if you actually do the basic requirements needed to complete your work and progress your career.

- **How well do you achieve goals?** Are you able to get your most important, core work done each week? Is your time constantly interrupted by irrelevant emails or calls? Do you achieve tasks ahead of schedule, or is everything handled at the last minute?

Understand your current situation

- **How well do you go 'beyond'?** Simply doing the tasks you are asked to do is one thing, but promotion comes to those who go beyond the regular duties. Are you providing creative ideas to your manager on a regular basis? Making it clear that you are a strategic thinker? Doing those god-awful internal programs which upper management love?
- **Are you holding relevant meetings?** Meetings are the primary time sink for office jobs, and people notice if yours are boring. Are you leading meetings well? Are the ones you attend a good use of your time? Do you speak up and provide useful input? Do you attend so many meetings that you get nothing done?
- **Are you networking properly?** Success comes from who you know, not what you know. Are you spending time with people outside your immediate job circle, who may help you with long term goals? Have you identified some of these people? If someone important contacts you, are you replying within a short amount of time?

Next you need to identify what others think of you – in particular if their opinion matches yours. So how do you find this out? It can be surprisingly difficult to determine, as many will refuse to give you clear feedback for fear of upsetting you. You'll need to be persistent, clear that you won't take offence, and able to read between the lines a bit:

- **Ask for informal feedback**: If you don't ask, you won't receive. Simple right? So make sure you actively ask others to provide feedback. The most effective way to do this is to ask informal questions after significant interactions with others (a large project, etc.) – this gives them something concrete to discuss.
- **Don't get offended**: You may be very surprised by the opinions that others have of you. Don't be defensive or react in a very negative way – you will only cut yourself from open feedback in the future.
- **Try objective tools**: There are a number of 'scientific' tools which aim to give a snapshot of your personality based on defined rules. Although the output is often less-than-reliable, the feedback can be easier to deal with as it comes from an objective source.
- **Be aware of the difference between behaviour and competence**: You will receive feedback on both of these, but there

is a difference between how you behave and what you are good at. The second is far easier to change than the first.
- **Look for patterns**: Look past feedback which you find insulting and attempt to see patterns in the responses. Do you see a consistent problem or strength which is being noted? If yes, then this is an area to focus on.

Understanding your organisation

Every organisation has its own culture – the mix of acceptable behaviours and attitudes which form the way 'things are done around here'. This can range from serious, conservative and hardworking (think of an old-school law firm) through to 'zany', relaxed and friendly (the stereotypical IT start-up). This culture is rarely stated outright, your colleagues will simply expect you to pick up the 'correct' behaviour by observation and copying.

Interestingly, there are generally *two* sets of office culture in place at any organisation. One is the 'official' one, promoted by management and reinforced by the office layout, décor, and general attitudes. The other is 'hidden', promoted by the colleagues themselves through their actions. The two rarely match, so you will often find 'relaxed' start-ups where no-one leaves before nine, or 'conservative' auditing firms where everyone is completely drunk by 5:30pm. Identifying these two cultures, then deciding how well you want to fit into them, is essential for enjoying your job.

How political is your organisation?

You cannot decide on your best approach before understanding the level of office politics currently going on in the workplace. This is a spectrum, running from minimal to insane, and you will find that it can vary wildly from department to department. In short, you can find the following main categories:

- **Minimal politics**: The group looks out for one another, arguments are quickly over, and there are no groups of insiders or outsiders. Rules are sometimes bent and people rarely play underhand tricks. This type of organisation is rare, but perfect for those who dislike playing the political game.
- **Moderate politics**: The organisation (normally a small one) operates on commonly understood rules. The focus is on results and teamwork, politics is used to bring good ideas forward and to achieve objectives – although this happens in a subtle and deniable

Understand your current situation

way. Conflicts are resolved using well-established rules or approaches.
- **High politics**: Conflict is everywhere, and it is solved by aggressive political approaches – the blame will be dropped on the loser, and they will normally be booted out. Formal rules are rarely used, usually only when they provide an advantage to the one who brings them up. There are clearly defined inside and outside groups, where *who* you know is more important than *what* you know. Life is stressful for everyone.
- **Insane politics**: No-one trusts anyone else, conflict is continuous and long-lasting. Very few people actually work, instead spending their time gossiping and spinning information to help their cause. Almost everyone works around the formal procedures, but make sure to cover their trail. Management thinks of their subordinates as idiots who need to be driven, not led.

The higher you move on the political intensity spectrum, the less productive your organisation will be and the more time they will spend on office politics and scheming. If your department is overly political, you will either have to learn these skills yourself or leave.

How do you know that you're getting into the dangerous area of an overly-political department? You'll see many of the following things:

- Blatant flattery of higher management, a refusal to say anything negative about superiors, and consistent abuse of those in lower positions.
- The only messages which are sent are heavily spun into something positive, and the only way to find the 'truth' is via rumours and gossip.
- Everyone gossips and backstabbing is common.
- People are not particularly valued for themselves, but seen as interchangeable parts in a machine.
- Teams and managers will happily lie about failures to seem good, and throw others under the bus in order to save their own career.

It's theoretically possible to reduce the level of politics present in the organisation. Successfully doing so requires a lot of effort – and to be honest will often fail in any case. It requires that management clearly and openly reward people for meeting their pre-defined targets, avoiding any hint that they are doing so out of favouritism. Similarly, they need to embrace the idea of open and honest communication (including bad news) and implement formal processes for making decisions on hot topics such as promotions, budgeting, and the like.

The challenge here of course is that those who deliberately try to be less political will be taken advantage of by those who are. In general it will only work when a politically-talented manager sets out to reduce the level of internal bickering – and this is often only achieved by firing the ones who get in the way of this plan.

Are you in a team?
One of the major factors which affects your strategy is the current situation you are in with respect to colleagues and team-mates. The best action for a lone expert in a solitary field is quite different to one who is in the middle of an overfilled team doing the same thing.

Having said this, you should be aware of the difference between a 'team' and a 'group'. If everyone is under the same manager, has similar roles, but nonetheless has very individual responsibilities, then you are looking at a working group. If everyone works on the same subject and shares responsibility, then it is a team. Although modern thinking tends to go on about the wonder of teams, they are not always the best option – particularly in cases where individuals need that personal responsibility.

How should you be perceived?
Interestingly, you don't actually have to be all that intelligent to go far in the office world. Or hard-working, or an excellent salesman, etc. But you need to have others *believe* that you are intelligent, or hard-working, or whatever your intended role is. Much of your overall success comes from presenting a persona to the corporation which fills one of their needs – this persona doesn't have to be accurate, but it needs to be in line with your goals.

What do we mean by this? Perhaps your department is looking for a high-flying expert in a technical domain, or a charming visionary on the newest innovations. This may not be in line with your personality, but acting as though it is your personality will bring you closer to the 'ideal' employee – and this ideal employee is the one who will receive the highest bonus and the first shot at promotion.

Understand your current situation

Thus one of your primary goals at this stage is to determine what personality traits fit best into the department and organisation as a whole. Once this is done, you can decide how to match these requirements.

What does your boss want?

It's pretty obvious that your boss (or direct manager) has a significant impact on your career. If they like you, you'll go well, if they don't, you won't. But it's more than simply being likeable, you need to understand their goals and objectives as well. Knowing their goals and helping to achieve them will do more for your relationship with the boss than any amount of friendly chit-chat.

The following lists a few things which you should determine now, as it has an impact on your later approach:

- **Their goals**: Just as you have goals which need to be achieved each year, so too does your manager. Your actions will (theoretically) help them to achieve these goals, and employees who deliberately focus efforts towards this tend to be highly valued and well-rewarded. We cover this in significantly more detail in a later section, but in general you won't go wrong by thinking 'what would I want to see, if I had a team member?'
- **Your role on the team**: Interestingly, managers often have a mental image of the 'ideal' team – the smart rookie, the abrasive expert, the quiet one who solves problems, etc. The composition of this team will differ between departments and between businesses, but the desire to have the perfect team is a strong one across all fields. Try to determine what your boss is looking for, what they are looking for in their fantasy team, and actively try to identify where you fit into this imagination. Once you have done this, map out what aspects of your behaviour or appearance you could alter to fit this fantasy more directly. Although becoming an obvious stereotype is a waste of time (and embarrassing), small changes can be very successful in becoming the star player on the team.
- **Whether they like you**: It's possible that your boss doesn't particularly like you, and in fact may be a full-blown psychopath or manipulative Machiavellian intriguer. We cover the typical displays of management madness in a later section, (page 125) offering some tips on how to spot them.

5. Managing initial impressions

It takes only a couple of seconds to create an impression of someone we have just met. And these impressions *last* – whatever you thought in that short moment will colour your feelings and interactions for a long time to come. It can be changed, of course, but it requires continuous effort to get new, positive messages in place.

Unfortunately, this is just as applicable to you as it is to others. Any negative impression you might give, that split-second decision made by others when they see you, will also last unless deliberately controlled. This means that you will need to put effort into controlling your image, particularly when you know that you will be meeting important people for the first time.

The first step in this process is to accept the necessity of managing impressions. Many people think of this as being underhanded, or sneaky, or somehow untrue. This is not the case – it is merely showing the world your *best* side rather than whatever side happens to be passing by. Corporations spend millions managing their major brands because they know how important these impressions are for success. You can do the same.

The importance of first impressions

You have probably heard the phrase "don't judge a book by its cover". This is a nice thing to say, but sadly makes no difference to how we act – everyone judges books by their covers, just as everyone judges the people they meet by their appearance. Still worse, these first impressions *stick*, they tend to remain present in our thoughts even after repeated interactions have shown them to be false.

Luckily we can also create a *good* first impression, not just a bad one. Furthermore, we can use our natural subconscious inclination towards mental short-cuts to extend these impressions to appear more competent as well.

So how do you use this to your advantage?

- Dress in a way which is consistent with the others in the organisation, particularly those in the position you *want to hold*.
- Your appearance matters. Observers will take your appearance and extrapolate from there to judge your overall competence.
- Learn how to shake hands. This seems minor, but it has a surprising impact on how you are perceived within the business world.

Managing initial impressions

What drives first impressions?

First impressions are made quickly and under pressure – there is no time to think and so our subconscious makes a snap decision based on all of the information it has available at the time. This requires a number of mental short-cuts and can often lead to a completely wrong outcome. At the same time, these mental short-cuts can be used as a way to *create* a specific impression in the mind of your counterpart.

The three main short-cuts which tend to occur in the office are the halo effect, stereotyping, and projection. All of these are quick to occur – you may find yourself being evaluated and pigeonholed within seconds of a meeting, and it will *definitely* occur within the course of the first conversation. You have one very short-lived chance to get your desired message across, which means that forward planning is essential. What do we mean by this? Here are a few examples:

- **The halo effect**: People latch onto one good personality trait or factor and then extrapolate from this to evaluate the rest of the person. For example, a charming smile at a first meeting will give the impression that you are honest and open, which in turn makes people believe that you are competent at your job – even though this is completely unrelated.
- **Stereotyping**: Stereotypes are generalised beliefs which we hold about others – for example, that all computer programmers have glasses and terrible style. Dressing and acting in a way which brings you closer to a desirable stereotype will often automatically create this belief in the viewer. The appearance and mannerisms of a 'successful' employee differ from organisation to organisation. What impresses managers in a hard-driving consulting firm will look different to those in a tech start-up, or a social-focused non-profit. If you can identify the 'target' stereotype of this successful employee, then modifying your look to match this will subconsciously influence those around you.
- **Projection**: We project ourselves onto others, and when we find a match (e.g. we both enjoy ice hockey, we both wear the same brand of shoe) then we automatically feel closer ties to them. This can be deliberately invoked when talking to others, most simply by wearing a similar (but not directly copied) outfit or carelessly name-dropping a shared hobby. Doing it well requires you to do some

research into their interests beforehand, and can backfire badly if you misread their interests.

Basic rules for the first meeting

The first meeting with anyone is an opportunity and a danger – in general you have a few seconds to provide an impression, and about five minutes to confirm it. Once that time is over, it takes significant effort to change the initial impression to something more favourable. So don't screw it up.

The following is a basic set of rules for a first meeting, it is generally more formal and may be more suited for job interviews or meeting higher management. But the general approach is suitable for all initial meetings, regardless of who is involved.

- **Don't relax in reception**: Take off your coat and leave it in reception, because carrying things into the room makes you look less professional. Don't take a seat, continue standing in a comfortable, confident pose – this helps to remind the receptionist that you are still there and still waiting.
- **Counter the waiting game**: If you have arrived on time, you should be in to see your contact within 5 minutes or so, longer begins to suggest disorganisation or an attempt to disorient you. Assuming you are carrying a laptop or work mobile, take it out and get some work done. When they do finally come out, pack up confidently and then follow them. You want to give the impression that the wait doesn't bother you, and that you can work through minor inconveniences.
- **Enter with confidence**: Once you get the go-ahead, walk in without hesitation. Don't pause in the entrance but keep walking at the same speed. This makes you look confident, as cautious or doubtful people will slow or halt at this point.
- **Approach confidently**: Walk directly and smoothly using a medium pace to your contact, even if they are on the phone or moving papers around. Smile, shake their hand, and sit. This clearly shows that you are used to walking into offices (i.e. you are a professional) and that you will not be kept waiting (i.e. you are important).
- **Shake hands**: We cover this in a later section (page 55), but in short: avoid shaking directly across the desk, instead try to step to the left of the desk to make it a handshake 'between equals'. Let

Managing initial impressions

them decide when to finish it. Use their name a few times in this first period.

- **Sit at an angle**: Try to turn the chair or your body so that you are slightly angled away from them (up to 45° or so will work). This avoids the direct face-to-face position which is so often associated with confrontation. Avoid sitting on a sofa (it makes you look small and weak), but if it is unavoidable then sit on the edge of the seat.
- **Clear, simple gestures**: Calm, controlled, and important people tend to use fewer gestures, and those they do use are clear, simple, and deliberately chosen. Try to do the same when talking to your contact, as this will subconsciously provide them with a better impression of your value.
- **Respect personal distance**: You will generally want to keep further back from people who you have just met, as they will instinctively be wary of you. If you see them leaning away from you or sitting back in their chair, this is a sign that you are too close. Move back a bit, relax.
- **Leave on a confident note**: When you are finished, pack your things in a calm manner without looking rushed. Shake hands and walk out, closing the door behind you (if it was closed when you first entered, naturally). You will *always* be watched as you leave, so ensure that your outfit is also presentable from the back, and turn around and smile/nod before you walk through the door. This ensures that they remember your face, not the back of your head.

Body language

Body language is a fundamental part of controlling first impressions. We've previously mentioned the importance of moving in a deliberate, calm, yet not too slow manner. Smooth, calm actions indicate confidence, and confidence is the most important impression to give others.

There are several other useful tips to remember as well:

- **Stand confidently**: Stand with your weight on both legs, keeping them roughly the same distance apart as your shoulders. Hold your head up – a helpful mental image is to imagine your head being pulled up into the sky by a cord. Don't shift your weight or your posture constantly. Avoid crossing your legs or folding your hands in front of you. This is a defensive pose, and confident people do not need to be defensive.

- **Eye contact**: Maintaining eye contact with people you are talking to is basically a requirement to come across as trustworthy or competent. Just don't overdo it, or you'll end up in the realm of creepy.
- **Talk with your hands, but not too much**: Use gestures (but not too much), as these help to keep your message across and get it to stick in the mind of your listener. Be careful of what you're doing though, avoid insulting gestures or those which imply you are close-minded.
- **Fingers closed**: Gesture with your hands, but keep them below your chin and keep your fingers closed rather than open. Even better, try to make a circle with your forefinger and thumb (the 'ok sign') as this keeps your hand in a closed configuration. This form of gesturing tends to draw attention and make you appear in control.
- **Don't fidget**: Fidgeting makes you seem nervous, nervous people are (funnily enough) not considered to be confident or competent by others. Don't fidget.
- **Clasp hands behind the back**: Clasping your hands behind your back while standing corrects your posture, pushes your chest out, and creates a pose which others instinctively associate with power and confidence. This is so ingrained that simply doing this pose yourself will influence you to feel more confident, even when nothing else changes.
- **Elbows out when sitting**: Sit in the chair, put your elbows out or on the arm rest. You take up more space and appear more confident.
- **Switch between angled and direct facing**: As mentioned above, sitting at an angle creates a more relaxed atmosphere which can help you create rapport with your counterpart. By contrast, directly facing them will create a confrontational atmosphere, which helps when you need direct answers to your questions. Switch between the two in accordance to your needs.

Dressing to match expectations

We tend to exaggerate the importance of clothes in our jobs (phrases such as 'clothes make the career' are dramatic but overdone). But how we dress *is* important, it is an outward expression of what we consider important and how strongly we want to fit in to the group. A good outfit won't save you

Managing initial impressions

from poor performance, but a bad one will certainly detract from your success. As a rule of thumb, it never hurts to err on the side of neater and more professional – even if you don't match the office style, you at least mismatch in the better direction.

Your target theme

If you're starting in a new role or company, your colleagues will be paying far more attention to you than usual. They will be looking for hints of your true working style, personality, and even your plans for the future. This, naturally, includes the way you dress.

The outfits you choose at the start of your new job, particularly if you are a team or department manager, tend to set the tone of your time in the role. Major changes from 'how we always dressed' can clearly signal that you aim to change the culture, even if this is not your plan.

All of this means you need to carefully plan your starting dress code. Generally you can choose from a few 'themes':

- **Quiet elegance**: Well-cut and fitted clothes, generally from expensive brands but which are not obviously labelled. This signals that you have money, but are used to it – money is no longer all that important.
- **Trendy and obvious**: Expensive clothes which are clearly labelled as coming from trendy designers or brands. This signifies that you are up-to-date with the modern world and not afraid to hide your interest.
- **Status quo**: You wear essentially the same thing as everyone else in the company. This is a clear decision to fit in with the crowd, and reassures onlookers that you (and your decisions) will follow the established rules.
- **Informal**: Your clothes are deliberately chosen to be comfortable and casual. This signifies the importance of informality and equality – it's the standard dress-code at most start-ups for a reason.

These are then further modified by the dress code which you find at your particular organisation – in general this is one of the 'main four': formal, professional, business causal, and casual. Note that none of these are exclusive to each other – just as the brand and style of a suit may change it from 'status quo' to 'elegant', so too can a hoodie and jeans. These different options are discussed in the following sections.

Business formal

This is the standard mode of dress which you see in high-level executives, those who regularly interact with them, or the legal field. You will sometimes hear it referred to as 'boardroom' dress as well, though this is less common in offices today. Regardless of the name, this is the most 'dressed up' you can be in business without going in a tuxedo or evening gown – and this in turn means that you have very limited options for creativity.

- **Men**: Have a fairly simple and well-defined set of requirements. You'll need a tailored suit in a neutral colour (black, grey, navy blue) and a white shirt. Ties can be more exciting, though stick to 'modest' styles such as single-colour ties or neutral, muted patterns. Shoes are generally brown or black oxfords, short hair is the standard, and the most exciting accessory you get is a watch.
- **Women**: Have similar requirements to those of men. Tailored suits (pant-suit or skirt) in the same neutral colour, generally with a conservative cut (i.e. skirts are about 2 fingers above the knee). White shirts/blouses, closed-toe shoes in neutral colours (often heels are expected, though not essential). Your hairstyle should be conservative, as should your accessories.

Business professional

This is slightly less formal than the previous level, though there is still the expectation that you dress conservatively and in traditional outfits. This is the 'everyday formal' of the business world, which means that you will need to have enough outfits to get through the entire week. To avoid dying of boredom, try to express your personality with accessories and by taking advantage of the wider colour choices allowed.

- **Men**: Again, suits are generally necessary, although at this level you can get away with conservative stripe patterns and the like (though colours remain conservative). You can also try dress pants and sports jackets, though this may get comments depending on the office. Ties remain conservative but can begin to include louder colours and patterns. Shirts can be blue, grey, or other dull colours. You watch should be metal, your shoes are still oxfords or loafers, brown and black remain the standard colours.
- **Women**: Suits or matching skirts/jackets in neutral colours remain necessary, though as for men your shirt can become more

colourful. Shoes remain neutral blacks or browns, but jewellery starts to become more noticeable – think single statement-pieces and the like. Hairstyles are usually flexible as long as it is neat and professional.

Business casual

This is the 'standard' dress code in most corporate offices and the one which you are most likely to come across. Business casual brings a more relaxed approach to styles and colour which allows you to add personality without immediately being written up. However, be aware that every company has their own idea of what is acceptable, so it's worth getting guidelines from HR before you go crazy with the colours.

- **Men**: Any colour shirt is acceptable at this level, as are conservative patterns (checks, stripes, etc.). Ties are generally optional at this point, though if you do wear one then it should have a conservative pattern (i.e. no piano keyboard ties, etc.). Dress pants are still required, and if it's cold then you can throw on a pullover (though again, make it a conservative colour and pattern). Shoes are flexible but should look formal, sneakers are going too far.
- **Women**: Can now start wearing separate items rather than full suits, and also have the option to wear basically any colour shirt or blouse (though avoid low-cut shirts). Shoes are finally comfortable at this level and can be any colour, though you should still stick to closed-toe. Feel free to use larger jewellery or a scarf, and hair styles or colours can be non-conservative, though neat is still necessary.

Casual

Casual is a difficult level to achieve, as there is a fine line between 'casual' and 'too casual'. Unfortunately even in a casual environment your colleagues will tend to judge your competence based on your appearance, which means that going too far will set your career back to some extent (although to a lesser degree as in a more formal office). Regardless of what you wear, make sure it is clean, neat, and suitable for the office.

- **Men**: Can wear casual pants, polos, sweaters and jumpers, with most colours being acceptable. If you want to wear jeans and hoodies, make sure that others in the office are doing the same (check with HR if you aren't sure). Sneakers and other casual shoes are fine at this level, but make sure they are clean. Hairstyles are now quite flexible, as are the accessories you can wear.

- **Women**: The general rule about 'nothing too revealing' also applies here, although there is a lot of freedom to choose colours, styles and fabrics. Open-toed shoes make an entrance here, though flip-flops are going a bit far. Casual or eye-catching accessories are fine, more colourful hair and nails are also ok. As with the other levels, make sure it's neat and professional.

A note on briefcases.

Briefcases are less of a topic in modern times, when most of us will be carrying around a laptop full of all necessary information, documents, and slide decks (though of course the modern equivalent would be a laptop bag or satchel). If you do have to work with printouts and hardcopy documents, then get some sort of professional-looking briefcase or case which allows you to carry everything together in a neat way.

Try to make it as thin as possible – there is a general stereotype that more important people carry thinner things. Walking around with a large, well-stuffed briefcase (or worse, a stack of folders balanced under your arm) gives the impression of an incompetent or unimportant office drone. This is, naturally, not good for your reputation.

Appearance matters

It's a bit of a taboo subject these days, as it makes a large number of people uncomfortable, but we're going to cover it briefly here regardless: Good looking people are far more successful in life than those who are not. This has been shown in numerous studies and is most apparent in sales-related positions (where your appearance helps to sell the product). However, as you have probably realised by now, office politics is *also* about selling things – your ideas, your competence, your value. Which in turn means that your appearance has a massive impact on your effectiveness within the office environment.

So what do you do about it? Appearance is difficult to change rapidly, obviously, but there are a few things which you can do that create quick improvements. Note that this is a short and (obviously) incomplete list, as we are not writing a book about makeovers.

Take care of your appearance

There are a few basic things that you should be doing in all situations to keep your appearance up to date. This doesn't mean working out, etc. (as

Managing initial impressions 53

we cover that later), but rather refers to the absolute minimum requirements which you need to be a professional worker.

What are we talking about? Things like:

- **Ironing your clothes**: Wrinkled, rumpled clothes are quite obvious in organisations with a higher level of dress code. The more formal requirements (ironed shirts, pressed pants, etc.) make your lack of effort stand out. This causes observers to extrapolate – if they can't even keep their clothes in order, they think, do I really trust them with my project? Avoid this career-killing impression by ironing and folding clothes, then storing them in a way that keeps them tidy.
- **Get a haircut**: Get your hair cut, comb it, and make sure it doesn't look like you just rolled out of bed. Seems simple, right? Yet somehow many, many people miss this and end up looking like teenagers on a bad day.
- **Slightly over dress code**: We went into the different dress codes in place in the previous section. In general, you should aim to be a tiny step above everyone else within the same dress code range. In other words, don't look like you are showing off, but try to look just that little bit more professional than your peers.
- **Shave or trim**: If you have a beard, make sure it's a neat beard. If you don't, then shave. Five o'clock shadows are great for the weekend, less impressive when your boss pops in with no warning.
- **Wash, shower, deodorant**: Yes, even more basic. Yet once again, a surprising number of people will miss this somehow-obvious requirement.
- **Smile and chat**: Aim to say hi to everyone you meet, give them a smile, and enter a conversation if they are interested. Small talk can be a chore, but it creates connections with others and helps build trust for the times when you really need it.

Exercising
Exercise is important. Do it.

The baseline recommendations from most health authorities are pretty simple. Aim for at least 150 minutes of moderate-intensity activity a week, (that's anything which gets your heart rate up and keeps it up – the usual definition is that you can talk, but not sing) or 75 minutes of high-intensity (can't talk, but can still breathe). You can split that time across multiple days, which means doing 30 minutes per weekday walking around at a fast clip will get you there.

In addition you want to do some sort of muscle-strengthening activity on at least two days per week. This might be lifting weights, doing push-ups and sit-ups, shovelling holes in the garden, rock climbing, or spinning on a stripper pole. It doesn't matter what it is, as long as you are working your muscles beyond their usual expectations.

This is (obviously) not a book about fitness, but there are a million different programs to choose from just one short web search away. Some need specialised equipment, others don't need anything but you. Spend some time looking around to find the best option for you and your lifestyle.

Eat well

There is a nice saying to the effect that muscle is gained in the gym, but weight is lost in the kitchen. Eating well is just as important to making a competent impression as any fitness plan.

Again, this is not a book about diet or the best meal plan to follow. You can find many, many options online, some useful, some useless. Most of it boils down to a fairly simple set of rules, particularly this one: don't eat too much, and make sure you eat a lot of fruit and vegetables. Figure out what works for you and implement it in your life.

Health at work

The daily office grind doesn't make it easy to stay fit – hours of meetings, sitting at the computer, or hiding in a cubicle take a daily toll on your health. Naturally you can't work out in the middle of the meeting room, but there are some very simple things which you can do on a daily basis to keep yourself on track.

- **Drink water**: Simple, right? No sugary drinks, no triple-martinis, just water. Bring a reusable bottle and fill it up – aim to drink the entire thing before lunch and after lunch. Keeps you hydrated, avoids headaches, and forces you to go to the bathroom often – so you get more chances to stand up.
- **Take breaks**: A nice rule of thumb is that you should stand up from your desk at least every hour. Go talk to a colleague, make a

coffee, swing by the bathroom – it doesn't matter what it is, the important thing is that you're moving around.
- **Never eat lunch at your desk**: Eating lunch at your desk is just a lost opportunity all around. Not only does it create an unbroken day of work (terrible for morale) but you miss any chance to network with other people in the company.
- **Don't slouch**: Sit up straight, pull your shoulders back, make sure the top of your monitor is level with your eyes. Get a real keyboard and stand for your laptop. Back problems are a terrible thing to have, so do your best to avoid them now.

Tattoos

The previous stigma of having tattoos is mostly gone from the workplace, particularly amongst 'younger' organisations or departments. Having said that, you will still find that there is some level of social stigma amongst certain groups – in other words, some people dislike tattoos and distrust people with them. These people also tend to be more common the higher up you go.

All of this means that means it can be helpful to cover up your artwork during working hours. This depends on what tattoo you have and where it is, but long pants, long-sleeved shirts, and clever use of accessories such as scarves or large watches can go a long way towards shielding it from view. Alternatively you can simply show it to the world, because the world likely doesn't care – just check with HR first if any policies exist, and be ready for some level of judgement.

Shaking hands

Although it sounds old-fashioned, the idea that a person can be judged based on their handshake is still very present in the corporate world. Given this it's worth putting at least some effort into developing a presentable handshake. Here are a few tips:

- **Say hello**: Handshakes without a verbal greeting are… well, strange. Say hello and mention your name just before you extend your hand – this makes the entire act part of one single business introduction.
- **Positioning implies dominance**: As a rule of thumb, the person whose hand is above the others is creating a show of dominance over the relationship. You can use this to either show your

importance to the other party (by forcing an overhand) or their importance (by accepting an underhand, for instance when apologising for a mistake). A neutral handshake has both hands aligned vertically, with the webbing between your thumb and forefinger in contact with theirs.

- **2-3 shakes**: You aren't pumping for oil, a handshake should be brief and to the point. If they won't let go, open your hand and spread your fingers – most people will recognise this symbol.
- **Reasonable force**: You don't want to crush your counterparts' hand, nor do you want a grip like a dead fish. Use about the same force that you would when pulling a door handle, and stay at that level even if they try to crush your hand.
- **One hand**: Two-handed handshakes are the realm of politicians, where they try to artificially appear friendly to those they have never met before. Don't do it. Unless you need to…
- **Disarm power-players**: The exception to the one-hand rule is when dealing with overly aggressive counterparts who extend their hands palm-down, attempting to force you into a submissive position. One way to prevent this is to start with a one-hand grip, then add your second hand to straighten the grip to vertical – this is a simple way to reassert control. An alternative involves accepting an underhand handshake and then stepping forward and slightly to the right towards them. This will automatically reorient the handshake to vertical, while the act of moving into their personal space acts to equalise the power-play.

6. Creating a competent reputation

Boring people are ignored, they sit in their cubicles and toil away for a lifetime of pointless servitude. You want more than that and therefore you need to *be* more than that. You need to have people notice you, talk about you, have you in mind when they are discussing projects and promotions.

As we discussed in the previous section, the impression you give to others is critically important. Even more importantly – it is often irrelevant how accurate this impression is. In other words, promotion and career doesn't come from *being* good, but from people *thinking* that you are good. Just doing your job isn't enough, you need to be keenly aware of the impression you create.

Assuming that you have passed the initial test and made a reasonable first impression, then it is now up to you to follow through. You need to act in a way which builds your long-term reputation with others in the organisation. They should picture you as someone to turn to when things are tough, who can be counted on to solve problems and avoid dangers without constant supervision. In other words, they have to see you as competent.

This chapter covers the various skills and approaches which you can use to solidify your long-term reputation. Specifically, it examines:

- Baseline minimum expectations which you need to meet to be considered competent (page 57)
- Tips and tricks for moving beyond and into the realm of 'an achiever' (page 61)
- Simple hints on how to manage your time, that most precious of resources (page 68)
- Using (and avoiding) meetings to gain maximum efficiency (page 69)

What are the baseline expectations?

A good reputation is generally built on being *better* than those around you. That means that there is a baseline level of competence which is required to even get started on this path. If you cannot meet the baseline, then you should worry less about office politics and more about developing your skills to the required level.

The following are a list of general expectations. These are somewhat focused on office jobs, but are broadly applicable across all careers:

- **Manage your time**: A basic skill for everyone, you should be able to manage your time and get the most important things done first.
- **Big picture awareness**: It's easy to put your head down and focus on nothing but your own little corner of the company. But it's expected that you'll be aware of the larger picture, seeing what's happening in other departments and using that to inform your decisions. This conveniently overlaps with developing political contacts, so you've really no excuse not to.
- **Make decisions on your own**: You can't avoid responsibility, particularly if you want any sort of rewarding career. So start now – start making decisions on your own, don't ask your manager for their opinion on every single decision. Tell them what you decided, of course, but do it later.
- **Think before escalating**: "Don't bring me problems, bring me solutions" – it's the stereotypical annoying manager phrase, but deep down *all* of them are hoping that you will act that way. Take a few minutes before you go to your manager and think of a few options to solve the problem. They may be completely wrong, but it's at least a first step.
- **Implement new programs and methods**: Be creative, think of new ideas or approaches, blatantly steal them from outside sources. Often your creativity will be shot down or mired in a bog of bureaucracy, but sometimes it will go though. Which makes a great impression on your superiors.
- **Teach**: New people start all the time. Help to teach them. Even if you're teaching them your job. Yes, your deep knowledge of your current role protects you from being replaced. But it also stops you being promoted, and who wants to keep the same job forever?

Beyond this, it's possible that you're a manager of some form. In this case there are additional expectations, mostly revolving around leadership. Here are some of the basic things you should be managing:

- **Delegate**: You have a team, and you need to use their talents to succeed. You can't succeed if you insist on doing everything yourself – even if you are better at it than they are. Only by

delegating effectively can you use the full talents of your team and avoid burning yourself out.
- **Set goals**: You are a leader, your job is to lead. How do you lead? Well, there are many ways, but one of these is to set goals for your team to aim for – this directs everyone's efforts and ensures that you are pulling in the right direction.
- **Make decisions**: There is nothing worse (or less respected) than a manager who doesn't make decisions. Stop hedging your bets, stop covering your arse with partial answers to your team's problems. Make a decision. Even if it turns out to be wrong later, you still need to make it.
- **Communicate well**: The manager's role is that of an information exchange – they need to pass things between their team, their peers, and their own managers. Give how important this is, you should obviously be able to communicate well.
- **Manage change**: Things change – new people start, new software comes in, the old department head is escorted out of the building, it can be anything at any time. And your people don't like change, it makes them worried. So a good manager will be able to guide people through change and uncertainty, easing their fears while preparing them for the inevitable.
- **Run meetings**: There are always more meetings. They'll take up most of your week, and each evening you'll wonder where the day went. So you should be able to run a meeting well, and actually get some value out of the damn things.
- **Motivate**: You lead in good times and in bad. And you need to keep your team enthusiastic about their work, even in bad times. So learn how to motivate.

What does your organisation expect?

There are a number of unwritten rules which exist in the workplace, you might hear them referred to as 'norms'. These are the expectations as to your dress code, how you deal with disagreements, the hours you work, whether you go out for drinks after work, whether you go for drinks *during* work, even whether dating within the office is ok or not. These rules are almost never explicitly stated, but you will nonetheless need to match these to succeed in the role.

What does this mean? Observe what people do, how they dress, how they act. Ask subtle questions of co-workers as to how you should act in certain situations. This is the workplace culture. It is ingrained in the company and exceptionally slow to change (much to the annoyance of new CEOs everywhere), and it is the main factor which will cause you to like or dislike your job.

Expectations don't just cover how you act, but how you perform your job and even what your job involves. Nor does everyone hold the same expectation – that would be too easy. The job description itself is generally a waste of time, so try to talk to all involved to find out what they want you to do. Write this down, make a list. Somewhere in the middle of it all is a better idea of what your job involves.

Of course, expectations only apply to your actions, not your thoughts. Feel free to be cynical about the latest bit of group-think or propaganda from global headquarters, just don't show it. Some colleagues will get away with ignoring these rules, they will either be very, very good at their jobs or very isolated from the main part of the company. You probably aren't the first, and hopefully aren't the second, so try to fit in.

Changing how you are perceived

It is possible that others do not see you in the way you would like to be seen – they see your weaknesses more than your strengths, perhaps they believe things which simply aren't true. Unfortunately, this doesn't actually matter – perception is *far* more important than reality when it comes to how people treat you.

This doesn't mean you're doomed to failure, it is absolutely possible to change the perception others have of you. The essential goal is to decide how you would *like* to be seen, how you are *currently* seen, and then determine a bridge between the two based on the values held by your target audience. To do this, we can use approaches developed by public relations experts (as the outcome is, essentially, the same).

There are a few general tips which you should keep in mind here:

- **Don't be overly ambitious**: Decide on one part of your reputation that you'd like to change, preferable something which will create an immediate win, and then focus on that. You should use the feedback you've been given and the needs of your job to pick out the most important facets to modify.

- **Don't lie... too much**: It is very difficult to persuade people that you are something you are not. Living a lie is very difficult to manage for long – you will inevitably get caught up by a small fact you never noticed. So ensure that the perception you are trying to project is as close to reality as possible.
- **Improve your awareness**: You should consciously try to assess how you affect others, how they respond to your actions, and what 'signals' they are transmitting to you when you interact.
- **Assess the values of your audience**: What do they find important or valuable? Do they prefer direct conversations, subtle dealings, are they afraid of conflict or love the challenge? This knowledge is required to tailor your change management program to their interests, as it is only by targeting the values of others that you will change their impressions of you.
- **Be visible**: Attempt to be part of strategic or important moments, particularly if it allows you to display the personality trait you are trying to fix in other people's minds. We tend to remember crisis situations better than the daily grind, and so your actions here will be worth significantly more to your overall perception.
- **Don't nag people for feedback**: They'll just start fobbing you off with excuses or pointless information. Similarly, you should not become emotional or defensive when people give you feedback – this will equally cause them to stop sharing with you.
- **Don't expect too much**: If you're well-known as the most evil guy in the building, there is a limit to what personality management can do to fix up your image.

Image management is about consciously targeting your audience with certain actions which will lead to a desired impression. To do this, you need to know who your audience is, generally higher management, your team, or the group you are looking to work with. You should be conscious of their values and what they consider important, and then adjust your style to meet that.

Moving beyond the baseline

Once you have the baseline requirements in hand, it is time to move onwards and start showing off your higher-level skills. Not developing these skills, but demonstrating them – simply doing your job isn't enough to get people to notice you. You need to *actively* create a strong and competent impression.

Thankfully most people are terrible at this, and thus there are some surprisingly simple things you can do to look amazing by comparison. A brief list is below, and we go into more important ones in the following sub-sections.

This includes:

- **Focus on important things**: There is a subtle but very important different between urgent topics and important ones, and you'll need to focus on the first of these. You will also need to anticipate what the future will bring, because what is 'important' can change in the blink of an eye.
- **Do the shit jobs**: Some parts of the job suck. Some suck because they are soulless wastes of time that no-one cares about, some suck because they are difficult tasks which *everyone* realises are difficult. Do the second one, not the first. Being known as the one who does that horrible task is the best way to quickly build a reputation as a hard worker.
- **Be patient, but not too much**: Take time to talk to others, understand their challenges and goals, find out how you can help them. Don't be afraid to spend some time in idle chatter to build up rapport. But don't be *too* patient – there are plenty of fools out there who will waste your time. Identify them and avoid them
- **Look like a manager should**: Be friendly, say hello and shake hands, smile with your eyes. Dress well, like you deserve respect and a promotion. Exercise, because fit people are better respected than the fat. As we mentioned in the previous chapter, appearance matters – and this doesn't stop after the first meeting.
- **Keep up with trends:** You should have an idea of what is trending in the world – this gives you a relevant and up-to-date impression. And you should be ready for the inevitable reversals of popular trends, as this often provides business opportunities.
- **Don't take stupid risks**: You need to take risks to get ahead, but they shouldn't be stupid ones. Check facts before passing them on, or making a decision based on them. Document everything, in meeting minutes or memos, to ensure that decisions can be traced

after the fact and that you will not be the sole scapegoat when things go wrong.

Speak rarely, speak well

People who talk continuously give off a less competent impression than those who talk rarely. Part of this comes from the rarity value – if there are only a few sentences spoken, then they are worth more than the flood of words from the next one. But it also comes from the slight sense of mystery – if others cannot immediately predict what you will say, then your input becomes that much more surprising and thus more valuable.

So how do you take advantage of this fact? Communicate clearly, focus on providing information which others can work with. Don't waste words, or force people to trawl through paragraphs of drivel to find the useful items. Don't be rude, of course, but try to be professionally clear in all your communications.

- **Limit personal sharing**: Yes, you have a personal life. No, it doesn't need to be broadcast to the world and your competitors. Be open but vague, happily speak in general terms but rarely in absolutes. This leaves a sense of mystery which keeps others guessing.
- **Calculate what you say**: Heard something and want to respond? Take a breath, wait a half second, whatever you want – just make sure you pause for a moment before you say something. Even a short pause is enough to second-guess a stupid comment, think of additional subtleties in the question, and better craft your reply. Others will also be aware that you are thinking about the response, boosting your intellectual reputation.
- **Calm in chaos**: When things go to hell, there will be a lot of shouting. Most of it achieves nothing. Remain calm, assess the situation, and *then* act – provide clear and well-defined instructions to those involved.
- **Get to the point**: If you have something to say, an important point to get across, then *say it*. Don't spend half a minute talking about irrelevant facts when you could be focusing on getting the vital information across.

Be confident

Confidence shows, and confidence impresses. Whether you're dating or managing, simply being confident in your chances will normally lead to success. This doesn't mean you should go for blind egotism and stupid decisions, (too much confidence leads to amazing screw-ups.), but rather than you should believe in yourself and your own talent.

A very simple way to achieve this is to actively focus on success. Why waste your time moping about the thousands of things which may go wrong? Plan for setbacks, naturally, but be confident that your chosen action is the right one, and that things will work out in your favour. Act this way even if, deep down, you do not believe it – it will still encourage your team and impress your observers.

In line with this is another simple rule: always accept compliments. If someone gives you a compliment, then accept it with a simple 'thank you'. Never try to deflect or downplay the compliment (i.e. "it was nothing") – this makes you look weak and insecure. Similarly, never 'match' by complimenting them in turn – this will look incredibly insincere. Simply thank them and move on.

Be energetic

Talent and skill will get you a long way in life, but their impact is nothing compared to your energy. Can you work hard and consistently, have you got the motivation to power through long days as you turn out amazing work? This is not to say that a long workday is the sign of success, rather that successful people are inevitably those who are not afraid of hard work.

With enough energy and strength, you can outlast or overcome those who are merely smarter or more talented than you are. At the same time, your endurance sets a role model for others in your team, encouraging them to work harder as well. The energetic, hard-working team quickly builds a reputation amongst the company, and you as the leader will get much of the credit.

Focus your efforts

Success comes from being competent, competence comes from experience. Spending your time switching wildly between one area of expertise and another ensures that you are mediocre at both.

This can of course be your plan – generalist managers do exist, and provided you build a set of broadly-applicable skills then you will be able to switch between roles and personas fairly easily. But every time you do this you will break off part of the network and reputation which you have developed so far. Contacts will slowly drift away, the new colleagues won't know about your previous successes, you will need to spend time re-evaluating the organisation and your position in it.

Although the usual approach is to change jobs at regular intervals, you should also look at the potential benefits to focusing your career on one industry (and for the brave, even in one company):

- You build up a solid core of sector-specific expertise, which makes you a valuable and recognised specialist in that area. This translates to higher wages, more freedom to make your own decisions, better exposure to upper management, and in the worst case a better chance at a lucrative consulting career later on.
- Your network-building efforts are similarly focused. You will build contacts with the important people in your field, and so will have more relevant help when you ask for it.
- There is rarely a completely new problem, it is often a variant on a problem which has occurred previously. This means you will often have solutions to the latest emergency simply by virtue of having seen it before (and this in turn builds your reputation).
- Upper management will know who you are, as you will create a consistent history of being involved in important events or projects. This smooths the career ladder and keeps your name in peoples' minds when discussing bonuses or fun postings.

Take smart risks

A purely risk-free career probably exists somewhere, but you are likely to die of boredom before reaching retirement. If you really want to move up in your field, you will need to show that you can succeed in uncertain situations. This means taking risks, making decisions based on limited information and with a chance of failure.

How do you show this?

- **Make decisions**: Obviously you can't take a chance if you never make a decision on your own. Step up, look at the options, and decide something for yourself. Hopefully it will work, maybe it won't. But you will never know unless you decide.

- **Don't be afraid of 'no'**: Many people feel an obligation to do things when asked, even when it isn't part of their job or even particularly important. Don't be like them. Say 'no' if the request doesn't fit into your long-term plans.
- **Try something new**: The 'usual way of doing things' is fine for general daily work, but if you want to improve performance then you'll have to try something new. So take a risk and bring in a new idea, a new process, a new set-up.
- **Be original, not correct**: You don't have to be correct on matters touching your speciality all the time, and even when you are most people won't pay attention. You are hired to be an expert there, after all, and that's just doing your job. But being inventive or original, particularly during a crisis – this is what will get you noticed.
- **Shit happens**: Sometimes your smart risk will crash and burn, leaving financial wreckage scattered across the company. Not great, obviously, but it happens. And when it does, you need to accept it and move on. Don't spend your time reliving the past.

Things will inevitably go downhill at one stage in your career, and you will have to deal with a stream of problems, challenges, and outright chaos. That's life, it's not easy, so deal with it. How you cope with adversity is one of the defining pillars of your career pathway – those who cannot manage will never achieve much at all.

What should you do when these situations arise?

- **Work on solutions**: This seems obvious, but there are many employees who simply pretend that everything is ok, that there is no need to worry, and who keep doing the same old thing while the project burns around them. Don't be this idiot. Actively work on solutions to your current problem.
- **Cut resources intelligently**: Sometimes you need to shrink budgets, cut projects, or even let people go. Never cut so far that you cannot return to normal operations once the crisis has passed. Make sure you reassure the best team members and keep them involved in the planning for recovery. Then give them lots of credit once the crisis passes. This is vital to avoid the top employees from moving to new roles during the problem times.

Creating a competent reputation

- **Sacrifice with the others**: If you are leading a group, and salary or benefit cuts are happening to keep the group afloat, then make sure your salary is being cut as well. And make sure *everyone knows it* – successful leadership is often based on symbols such as this.
- **Sacrifice the others**: Of course, sometimes it will come to a situation where it really is you or your team. If you have a clever exit strategy lined up which you can bring closer through self-sacrifice, then by all means go for it. If not, well, drop the others. Such is life in business.
- **Plan for success**: Your solution should hopefully bring the project or group beyond the point it had at the start of the crisis. In other words, don't aim to return to 'how things were before', try to improve.

Don't do stupid things

It seems obvious, but your reputation will take a dive if you do stupid things. It will take even more of a dive if you do the things which *everyone* knows are stupid.

Here are some of the very obvious stupid things which you obviously shouldn't do, and which obviously I don't need to mention. And yet, somehow, people still forget that they are stupid things to do:

- **Being racist**: Don't make others feel uncomfortable based on their ethnicity or skin colour. This means not doing the blatant things (racial slurs, jokes, insults) and not doing the subtle things (e.g. insinuating that a promotion only came to fill a quota).
- **Being sexist**: Don't change your treatment based on the others' gender, don't bias promotions in favour of one or another gender, don't make comments about women staying at home in the kitchen.
- **Harassing others**: Whether it's bullying or intimidation, pressuring other employees or even just viciously micromanaging another, harassment is a bad idea and will come back to bite you at some stage.
- **Behaving inappropriately**: You're a professional, act like one. Don't swear, don't make inappropriate jokes, dress well, wash yourself, and shave that damn neckbeard. Think about the other employees, and what they'd expect from you.

All of these are blatant career killers, particularly in a modern office environment. Although you can (very often) get away with this for a long time, it will eventually come back to haunt you. Particularly as they make very convenient political weapons for your enemies. Save yourself the trouble and watch your behaviour today.

Managing your time

No matter who you are, no matter how far up the hierarchy you have managed to climb, you will only have 24 hours in the day. This hard limit means that those who are most effective at managing their time and attention are the ones who will achieve the most. And this, in turn, leads to career success.

So how do you manage your time well? There are a million books on this subject, but here are a few simple rules to follow:

- **Delegate**: You will have a lot of tasks coming across your desk. But you don't need to do all of them – and indeed trying to do so is a recipe for failure. Repetitive tasks, tasks with limited impact, tasks which are neither urgent nor important – these should be delegated to other people.
- **Screen**: Most of the emails you receive will contain no information, most of the meeting requests you receive will be a waste of time. Screen calls, emails, and visitors and ruthlessly dump the ones which are not important. Archive information if you have to, but be aware that you will almost never go back to read it a second time.
- **Prioritise**: If it's urgent and important, do it now; if it's important but not urgent, do it next; if it's urgent but unimportant, then delegate it; and if it's neither urgent nor important, then ignore it. The challenge then lies in deciding what should be considered urgent and important...
- **Have a to-do list**: Keep track of your tasks, use some sort of system which allows you to group them and reorganise them when more important priorities come in. Never assume that you'll be 'able to remember it' – you have too much to do to waste time remembering things. Write it down.
- **Schedule your day**: Use your calendar. Block off time where you need to focus on particular tasks, and make sure that ~10% of your day is blocked off for spontaneous visits or problems. Revisit your schedule at the end of the day and decide if you were efficient or

Creating a competent reputation

not – could some of those recurring meetings be dropped or reduced?

- **Have efficient meetings**: Meetings can suck vast amounts of time out of your day, often for no real gain. If you organise a meeting, make sure it starts on time – cut off latecomers if you need to. If you receive an invite, make sure there is a topic and agenda for the meeting – if not, then request one be sent out. Leave when the meeting time is up, even if they are still waffling on (you can always claim another meeting is pressing). Some further tips for controlling meetings are presented in the following section.

- **Put off consistent meeting requesters**: Some people are in love with the idea of meetings, they will constantly organise a session to align on details, discuss the latest updates, or just chat. This is a waste of your time. Generally you can offer a slot for discussion in the semi-distant future ('next week' tends to work well), by which stage the need for 'urgent' discussion should have passed.

- **Turn meetings into spontaneous chats**: Meetings can be difficult to finish prior to their defined end time, even if the discussion topic is at an end. This is particularly problematic if the meeting is in your office, you will either have to throw them out (which isn't good, politically) or wait until the time is up (which wastes your valuable time). To avoid this, try to meet others in their office or at their desk. Coming to them gives an impression of respect and interest in their well-being. It also makes you the 'visitor', so you can leave whenever the discussion topic is at an end. You can even 'coincidentally' pass by their desk a few hours prior to the meeting, and ask if you can quickly discuss the topic now. The answer is usually 'yes', and it is always faster than a formal meeting.

Being efficient with meetings

Once you hit a certain point in the company, the majority of your time will be spent in meetings. Meetings within the department, with other experts outside the department, with randomly irritating salespeople from other companies – regardless of the people involved, you will be sitting there and talking, having a meeting.

Meetings aren't evil by themselves, of course, they are a great way to get decisions made or to ensure that you're all thinking the same way before doing something important. But too many people call a meeting 'because they can' — because they want to show off in front of others, are scared to take a decision alone, or simply want the chance to chat. This is a waste of your time and the time of everyone involved.

There are several approaches you can use to dodge unwanted or unnecessary meetings, as described in the following section. Those meetings which you do need to attend (or even run yourself) can be made fast and efficient. As meetings are a universal problem across all levels, others will notice and value you for doing this well. In fact, few things will build your corporate reputation as much as being the person who runs a quick meeting which *gets things done*.

Spotting and avoiding pointless meetings
The first stage to avoiding pointless meetings comes at the very first moment, when the email invitation arrives in your inbox. You should already be able to see if this meeting will be worthwhile or not, simply by looking at the person who sent it, the title, and the information in the body. Here is a very simple way to determine if a meeting is worth attending:

- You will be making a decision which affects multiple people, and need to get opinions and alignment.
- The meeting will provide strategic information regarding one of your projects or even the company as a whole.
- You would like to strengthen relationships with the people involved via face-to-face interactions.

If a meeting invitation cannot meet one of these three requirements, then it is a waste of your time and should be avoided. This is particularly true for the 'update' meeting, where people will provide a description of what they have been doing lately. Updates do not require a meeting, simply send around an email with a summary — and just like that an hour of everyone's time is saved.

Avoiding meetings is, unfortunately, not easy. The first step you should take is to make the act of inviting you just that little bit more challenging for others. 'Friction' plays a very strong role in all of our interactions, in that even the smallest added difficulty will cause a significant drop in motivation. For example, hiding your calendar makes it a little bit harder for others to plan meetings around you, which means they will often exclude you from the list (or invite you anyway, at which point you can reject the invite and claim a prior appointment).

Creating a competent reputation

You should also force meeting organisers to provide information on the topic to be discussed. Simply reply, politely, asking for a meeting agenda, the decision which needs to be made, and what information or input you are expected to provide. If you are necessary, you now have a much better idea of what will occur and can plan accordingly. If you *aren't* necessary, you can point this out and suggest a short phone call, an email summary, or even schedule a follow-up for a few weeks in the future (by which time they will have forgotten all about it).

If you are truly being forced to attend a meeting with low importance (often by your manager or, still worse, a 'matrix manager'), make it clear to those involved that it requires a trade-off. Say that you are quite happy to attend, but you are also working on Task X. And ask if they are ok with you deprioritising this task in favour of the meeting. Assuming this task is genuinely important (which it should be, else why are you doing it?) others will often excuse you from attending.

Attending relevant meetings

If you have decided that the meeting is really worth your time, then you need to make sure that you are getting the full value out of it. In particular, attending a meeting while not saying anything is simply a waste of time. And worse, it robs you of the chance to impress the others with your knowledge, leadership skills, and other fine talents.

This means it is vital to speak up during a meeting, particularly in the first 10 minutes or so (otherwise no-one will remember that you were there). Speaking up can be daunting, of course, particularly in large meetings or those with higher management, but is an essential part of career development. This doesn't mean that you should just say any old rubbish which pops into your head. Instead, you need to craft your presence and commentary in a way which paints you in the best possible light.

Here are a few helpful tips which may help:

- **Don't be late**: Everyone remembers the one who comes in late to the meeting, and they won't remember you positively. Plus you'll miss out on the pre-meeting chatter, which is often more informative than the meeting itself.
- **Prepare beforehand**: Don't try to 'just wing it' at the meeting, hoping that you'll be able to make up some clever answer on the spot. It rarely works, and most people will realise that you're doing

it. Instead, prepare beforehand. Look at the agenda, spot items which you will likely be asked to comment on, think up likely questions to ask and which you may be asked. Plan and develop answers as needed – this will look very impressive if you are put on the spot.

- **Talk, don't read the slides**: The business world is full of terrible presentations given by office drones who simply read their (badly) pre-prepared slideshow. These people are quickly dismissed as insignificant by upper management, even though they may be highly talented in other roles. Don't do this. *Present*. The audience should be focused on you, because that is what they should remember.

- **Yes you can**: Don't undersell your importance – you were invited to the meeting for a reason, and you accepted it because the reason was a good one. This means that your input is valued by the others, so don't be afraid to express it!

- **You don't always have to say something**: If you have nothing useful to say, it's better for everyone involved that you stay quiet rather than making up some pointless question and derailing the conversation. If you are asked to give an opinion, make it clear that the others have already expressed your thinking. This allows you to skip commenting, while still giving the impression that you are fully involved in the meeting.

- **Have a back-up plan**: Sometimes you'll be asked something out of nowhere, generally at a time when you weren't paying attention at all. Have a few sentences in reserve to buy time to find an answer – think of comments such as 'could you provide some background information?', 'I can't answer that right now, but will let you know by X o'clock', or 'here's how I understand the issue so far, correct me if I'm wrong'.

- **Complain in the meeting, not in the corridor**: You'll be in many meetings trying to get decisions made. This is the time to make your viewpoint known and hammer out a consensus. If it doesn't go your way, don't complain about it later in public – this will give you the reputation of a whiny sore loser. Instead, discuss it subtly in smaller rounds, using your contacts and influence to try and recast the decision.

Creating a competent reputation

Run an efficient meeting

Running an efficient meeting is difficult – doubly so when it is full of uninterested attendees who don't really need to be there. Follow the tips in the previous section to ensure that you only hold meetings with a valid reason, and that you only invite the people who need to be there. Once you've done this, you can then add several more approaches to ensure that it is efficient and effective – this will cement your reputation as a good organiser.

- **Provide an agenda**: Meetings without an agenda rapidly drift off into pointless discussion about topics which were already discussed to death the last three times. Any meeting invitation you send out should have a clear agenda, and this agenda should be summarised at the start of the meeting to remind everyone why they are there.
- **Minimise attendees**: The more people in your meeting the less it will achieve, with groups of less than seven working most efficiently. The only people in your meeting should be those who are directly involved in the decision to be made – either to provide information, implement the outcome, or make the decision itself. It should be clear when you put the invitation together who those people are.
- **Sit at the head of the table**: Even if you do nothing else to exert control over the meeting, do this. The person sitting at the head of the table is automatically and subconsciously seen as influential by the others – their opinions are considered more valuable, their topics more worthwhile.
- **Make a decision**: There are few things worse than a meeting which covers old ground, or reopens a decision which was made months ago. Keep track of decisions which are made during meetings and the consequent implementation plans, then follow up to see if these were done. Keeping records forces at least some accountability into a meeting or steering committee. This also applies to one-off meetings, where you should have a formal record of the meeting which includes the decision and outcome.
- **Don't overdo the slides:** Many formal meetings will have some sort of PowerPoint slide deck, either as detailed pre-read information or for presentation during the talk. If you are responsible for preparing them, make sure that you have a self-contained 'summary' section which provides all the important info.

Feel free to throw everything else into the backup section, but the slides itself should be quickly done so that you can go on to the decision-making part.

Facilitating meetings

Some meetings are yours to make the decision – you are discussing with your team, you are the main person involved in this topic, you are the one who will get blamed and so are trying to get some help. In all of these cases, you'll need to facilitate the meeting, keeping the various participants on track and (hopefully) with a reasonable outcome at the end.

There are a few major points to remember when facilitating:

- **Sit at the head of the table**: The person at the head of the table is subconsciously considered to be the most influential one there by the others, even if everyone is nominally the same rank. Use this effect to improve your control over the group.
- **Stay calm**: Meetings can get nasty, especially when something went wrong and people are trying to pass on the blame. Take a deep breath, count to 5, or 10, and then carry on. Anger may make you feel better, but it rarely helps solve problems – and worse, it makes you look incompetent.
- **Don't take sides until the end**: There will be arguments (or at least disagreements) and the meeting will coalesce around several different approaches, each of which will have a main representative. Let them argue out the pros and cons, make sure the opinions of all involved are included. But don't express your opinion until the end, when everyone has said their piece. Because as the facilitator your opinion automatically carries a bit of extra weight, and it is important to let the others discuss freely. Note that this only applies if you want open discussion – if you want to drive the decision in your chosen direction, then say your preference up front.
- **Send an agenda**: There's nothing worse than a meeting invite with no topic or agenda – do you accept or reject it? Why am I invited? What the hell are you going to be discussing? Save your attendees these questions, and their irritation at you, by sending an agenda with the initial invite.
- **Keep to the agenda**: Keep the meeting on track, even if your people try to wander off and discuss completely pointless or irrelevant topics. Sometimes these are helpful, but if it takes more

than a few minutes then you should point this out, schedule a follow-up meeting on that topic, and get back on the agenda.
- **Start and end on time**: This is pretty simple. You have a number of people in a meeting room, they all have a lot to do. They don't want to sit around waiting for the one last person to turn up. Nor do they want to site there after the meeting time is over waiting for a long-overdue decision to be made. So start and end the meeting on time.
- **Encourage participation**: Everyone should get involved, everyone should share their knowledge and experience. Your job is to nag the quiet and tell the loud to shut up, so that all the voices can be heard.

7. Become known as a decision-maker

Eventually, a time will come in your career when you will have to make a decision. Many people try to go their entire lives without making a job-related decision, keeping their heads down and simply watching as events pass them by, hoping not to be noticed. These people make up the majority of most corporations and can be safely considered irrelevant by anyone with serious career aspirations. You, by contrast, should get used to making decisions – because nothing boosts visibility and promotion like a reputation for making the *right* decision.

Note that we say the "right decision" because failures don't get promoted. Which means you have to think about what you are going to do *before* you do it.

Questions to ask yourself

Before you do go about making a decision, there are a couple of important questions which you should ask yourself:

- How is this decision relevant to what I do? Am I the best person to make the decision?
- What specifically would I do?
- What would be considered 'successful' in this regard?
- What do I have to support my actions?
- Do I have enough information to make a decision?
- How can I mitigate a lack of information?
- What would be the worst possible result if I make that decision?
- Do I need to make a decision at this time?

How is this decision relevant to what I do?

Presumably you have a job with some sort of fixed responsibilities and expected results. Your manager will have certain expectations, and one of those is that you deal with problems within 'your area' of influence. In other words, if you are hired to co-ordinate logistics of raw materials, then you should be making decisions which lead to success in that role.

But sometimes you aren't the right one for the choice. Maybe the consequences are too high-level for your pay grade, in that they affect the future of your department or company. Perhaps it is a strategic choice, maybe it's outside your area of expertise or responsibility. It's pointless

Become known as a decision-maker

deciding something only to have it overruled by your immediate supervisor, and career-destroying when the CEO needs to ask why you made this decision without escalating the information to him.

So whenever a decision does come up, you should ask whether you are *really* the right one for it. Don't look to pass the buck, but genuinely try to decide if this is part of your assigned responsibility and power. If it is, then make the decision. If it rightfully should be made by someone else, then pass it on to them.

What specifically would I do?

It's rare for a decision to come in clearly-defined terms, particularly when it's an important one. Perhaps you'll get a quick message asking you to 'fix something', or (far worse) be forwarded an email chain with some cryptic comment like "we should do something here". You cannot make a decision if you don't know what you will be deciding between, and thus your first priority is to determine what is at stake and what the potential approaches could be.

What would be considered 'successful' in this regard?

You want to succeed, oddly enough, and so you need to determine what 'success' will look like. Will this decision lead to increased income, better conditions, or even just replace a major failure with a minor one? A single crisis may require you to decide between multiple different approaches, each of which will have their own success and failure outcomes. Which of these is closest to the success criteria which your manager uses? Their manager? The CEO? Knowing how you will be judged for your performance is an important part of making politically-successful decisions.

What do I have to support my actions?

It is rare that the outcome of a decision is purely dependent on your willpower and your actions. In almost all cases you will have to work with others, tap into external information sources, or persuade management to give up some of their time or money. The availability (or lack) of these resources can change your options, which in turn affects what your final decision will be. If you have serious resource constraints, then it may be necessary to solve this problem first before you can move onto the real problem.

Do I have enough information to make a decision?

You will never have a perfect overview of all the factors which will lead to your success or failure. Or rather, you may eventually have this overview, but it will be too late to take advantage of the moment. You will need to become comfortable with making decisions based on imperfect information, using a combination of knowledge, experience, and risk mitigation to maximise your success.

This doesn't mean you should make decisions blind, guessing the path to take by throwing darts or flipping a coin. Sometimes there will simply not be enough information available, rendering any decision you make the equivalent of blind luck. If this is the case, *don't decide anything*. Figure out what you would need to know, then go and figure out where that information might be. Only make the decision when you have a fair idea of what the consequences might be – anything less is setting yourself up for failure.

How can I mitigate a lack of information?

As famously said – the true challenges are the unknown unknowns, the things which we don't know, need to know, but are unaware of the fact that we should know them. As these tend to be the most important factors in any outcome, you should at least try to identify what they are.

But often you will not have the option to do this, particularly in a high-pressure situation where a fast decision is needed. But you can at least try to mitigate the lack of information by your actions:

- If you have possible options which seem uncertain, or where knowledge is limited, then try putting a low-risk, simple attempt into place. It may fail, but will do so cheaply, hopefully helping to spot potential challenges along the way.
- Make the decision, but determine checkpoints before you implement it. These are fixed, pre-defined points at which you will reassess the newly-available information and decide whether the current approach is the best one.

What would be the worst possible result if I make that decision?

Speaking of failure, it helps to think about the worst possible outcome that may occur. The 'absolute failure', as it were. This is helpful for several reasons. First, it lets you determine upcoming risks and put mitigation actions in place. Second it acts as a handy booster for your courage – sure, things may go wrong. Probably will. But the worst possible outcome is often not as bad as you think.

If you are in a highly uncertain situation, there are several approaches you can take to maximise your success:

- **Reduce the time horizon**: Long-term outcomes are difficult to predict, and worse in complex situations. Rather than taking one big step into the unknown, determine short-term actions which you can take to maximise flexibility in the future.
- **Keep options open**: Having multiple options or approaches to deal with a problem allows you to rapidly switch if further problems arise. You can then narrow down the options as more information comes in. This often takes more effort than simply making a choice and going for it, but significantly improves your chance of overall success.
- **Improve knowledge and classify risk**: Gain as much information about the different options as you can. Use this to estimate the associated risks, as well as the probability and impact if they occur. Decide what the worst-case outcome might be. This makes you more familiar with the possibilities, and thus less afraid of taking a new approach.
- **Minimise risky situations**: If you are faced with an uncertain situation, but are able to control the timing of other risks, then place them on hold while the main problem is worked out. Similarly, you should avoid having multiple risky situations occurring simultaneously – take them one at a time if possible.
- **Remain flexible**: Don't become overly attached to one approach or another – be ready to change your approach as new information comes in.

Do I need to make a decision at this time?

Just as you need to have the right information to make a decision, you also need to know that you are choosing the right time to make a decision. Perhaps there is vital data which will only be available two days from now. Perhaps a major decision is about to be made on another project which will free up resources for you to use. In both of these cases it makes no sense to decide anything *now*, because the upcoming information may completely change your strategy.

The challenge is figuring out when the decision should be made. Too early, and you miss out on valuable information. Too late, and you will find that the number of available options rapidly decrease. Although it's impossible to precisely pick the right moment for a decision, there are a number of biases which will push you one way or another. If you can recognise these in yourself, then you can try to consciously push the other way.

People who make decisions *too quickly* tend to make these mistakes:

- They make impulsive decisions based on an emotional basis, without gathering information.
- They consider early events as more significant than later ones, which pushes them to make decisions based on this 'more important' information.
- They prefer immediate outcomes or payoffs compared to later ones.
- They downplay or disregard risks when making decisions.
- They use 'shortcuts' in decision-making, relying on easily-obtainable information or things which 'everyone knows' to make a decision.

Those who tend to decide *too late* often have the following biases:

- They try too hard to gather information, including data which cannot affect the outcome, or focus on the process of gathering information rather than the information itself.
- They procrastinate, deciding that they work can be done later.
- They consider recent events as more significant than earlier ones, which leads them to delay for more information.
- They ignore the possibility of 'novel' events occurring, and are surprised when they do occur.

Delaying a decision can be very tough, particularly when you have people screaming at you to figure something out and get your team moving. If you are confident that waiting is the correct option, then hold on to that belief. Discuss it with others, and show them why you need to wait. But be prepared for a lot of nasty comments, even if you turn out to be correct in the end.

The decision-making process

So you've put on your grown-up pants and you're ready to do something exciting – you're going to make a decision. Presumably you're doing so in an uncertain situation, with a lack of good information and many different possible outcomes (because if it was an easy situation, you wouldn't need any help).

There is a fairly simple set of steps which you should follow when making decisions. It should be noted that the steps themselves are simple to explain, but implementing them successfully is far more challenging.

Essentially, you should:

- Frame the decision within your situation
- Brainstorm many different ideas
- Decide what to do and commit to this
- Manage the risks, consequences, and communication

Frame the decision within your situation

Every decision happens within its own set of circumstances. Important decisions, ones which can boost your career, usually have a unique set of circumstances – after all, if it were familiar, you would not have to worry about the outcome. Your first task is to figure out what situation you are in, and how you can manoeuvre within it to achieve your goals.

What does this mean? You should be able to determine answers to the following:

- What are the causes and compounding factors of the problem?
- What 'needs' are in play that will need to be addressed?
- What will you consider to be a "success"? Can you identify specific criteria which need to be met by any successful solution? (Often these fall under the heading of performance, schedule, cost, compliance, and consistency). If there are multiple factors, how are these balanced? Are some more important than others? Can you create a prioritised list?
- Who are the stakeholders in the decision? What are their motivations and involvement? Who is impacted by the decision? Who would like to be informed? Who has a very strong interest in everything turning out one way or another? And who doesn't really care, but needs to be included for political reasons?

- What information is available now? What will be available in the future? What will never be available? (Or at least, not within the required timeframe) How will you get this information?
- What is the 'value' of the decision – are you talking about a few dollars or a few million?
- How much of your time should be devoted to this decision? (This strongly correlates with the value)
- When do you need to make the decision? Do you have enough time, or is it a rush job?
- What other decisions will feed into this one? Or have you previously made a decision in the past which will reduce (or increase) your options here? If so, can you go back and change this decision?

Once this is in place, then it's time to start generating new ideas.

Brainstorm many different ideas

Once you have an idea of how your problem fits into the current situation, then you need to think up alternative options to pursue. Generally the more creative you are at this point the better the final outcome – if you've a choice of two options, then you should go back and think up some more. The ideal number is between 5 to 9 options – any less and you lose flexibility, any more and it becomes hard to evaluate and make a final decision.

Thinking up new ideas is obviously a bit more complicated than that. It's important to remember that you don't have to invent a *completely* new solution to your problem. Many problems are just a new spin on an old challenge, and you can do the same with your solutions by taking previously-developed ideas and repurposing them for the current situation. Generally these fall into one of three categories:

- **The same solution as last time**: If the *problem* is the same as one you've seen in the past, and there is no need (or interest) in trying something new, then why not use the same *solution* as last time?
- **Options you looked at last time, but rejected**: If the problem has come up in the past, you probably (hopefully) looked at a number of different possible solutions. As circumstances change, many of these previously-rejected options may now be worthwhile or even the better option. Bring them back in and evaluate them

again. This is also an excellent reason to keep a permanent record of your evaluations and eventual decisions.
- **Options made for a similar decision in different situations**: You will often find that a similar problem has occurred in a slightly different situation, department, or environment (or even a completely different industry). The solutions for these problems can usually be reworked to fit your specific circumstances, with the added bonus that you already have an example to follow.

But you cannot simply work from previous ideas, you also need to brainstorm new and potentially better alternatives. This is best done by building off the information you already have, as in the following:

- **Create hybrids**: Figure out the different component pieces of your previously-identified solutions. Then mix these parts together to make a new hybrid approach.
- **Fill gaps**: Each of your success factors can be thought of as a range of acceptable options in the middle of a long list of unacceptable outcomes. Look for two solutions which fulfil the opposite edges of this acceptable range, and try to create a mixture which fills in the gap.
- **SWOT**: A standard technique, you need to assess the strengths, weaknesses, opportunities and threats inherent in your known solutions. Now build off that and look for approaches which enhance the positive aspects.

By this point you should have come up with a number of different options, probably more than you really need. Too many options leads to bad decision making – there are so many alternatives that we cannot keep track of them, and so default to things which feel familiar even if they are not the best options.

What does this mean? Now is the time to reduce the number of options for assessment – you should be aiming for 5-9 different alternatives. Here are some quick tips:

- Look at your key success criteria – do some of the options not meet this requirement? Then boot them out for being infeasible.
- Think of higher-level decisions which will reduce the field. For example, if you only have a certain budget, then every option which exceeds this can be removed from the assessment (unless it is a

particularly amazing approach which you can astound management with, which does happen on occasion).
- Narrow the scope of your decision by first deciding on a strategic approach you will follow. This allows you to exclude options which don't follow your required strategy.
- Combine options with minor differences, or those where the differences do not impact your need/want requirements.

Once you have reached this point, it's time to move on to the next step – evaluation.

Decide what to do and commit to this

Now that you've put all of these alternatives down on paper, it's time to evaluate them. Take the important factors you determined in the previous steps, and write down the impact of each alternative on these factors. If you cannot say for certain (as is often the case), then include your best guess and some information on how reliable this is (firm assumption, possible, half-arsed guess, etc.). Do this for all options and all factors and you will normally end up with a large table full of information.

In a bit more detail, this would involve the following:

- Copy the criteria for success and your different alternatives into a table – most people use Excel spreadsheets for this, there are plenty of templates out there. Regardless of your choice, you should be able to give scores for each criteria in each alternative.
- Ensure that any new issues which have popped up during the evaluation have been included in your decision-making criteria.
- Collect and classify the information which you need to evaluate each criteria. Try to use unbiased, comprehensive sources of information, though if a source is known to be biased then you should aim to use the same source to evaluate all alternatives. This means that the data itself is biased, but you can compare your options. Regardless of the data source you use, you should record how reliable it is – this helps with your assessment later on.
- Look at each criteria, and define the 'must' requirements (what it absolutely needs to fulfil) and the 'want' requirements (those you would like to have). This should be assessed for each of the possible alternatives.

Become known as a decision-maker

By this stage you should have an idea of how 'good' your options are. Does one of them stand out as a clear winner? Are others tempting, but have significant risk associated with them? Do some alternatives match up with other opportunities which you would like to follow, providing you with a two-for-one benefit? And can some of them be discarded right away based on their terrible outcomes? In tough situations where it is difficult to find the right path, simplifying the decision space by removing options is often a good first step.

These questions seem simple enough but are inevitably complex in practice. There are no lack of methods for making decisions (from flipping a coin up into the heights of complexity), but a good option is known as "multiple criteria decision analysis", or MCDA. This is an inherently simple approach which can be scaled to meet the complexity of almost any decision

- The first step of the process is to evaluate each of your options against the 'must have' criteria you identified before. Any option which doesn't meet this level can be booted out of the evaluation, saving you effort and preventing the analysis of hopeless alternatives.
- The second step is to look at each option and how it fulfils the 'want' criteria. Make sure you evaluate the performance of all options against each criteria – this avoids you unconsciously biasing towards one option by 'accidentally' ignoring an important factor. You should try to estimate how well the option fulfils (or surpasses) the criteria for later comparison. It also helps to start with the most-important criteria first – you will inevitably run out of time halfway through, and doing this will at least keep you focused on the most important factors.
- Now look at the risk and opportunity associated with each of the options. An option with an excellent *potential* outcome but a high risk of failure is often worse than one with a less-exciting but almost-certain outcome.

Assessed everything? Then it is time to select the option which best meets the success criteria and risk requirements. Easy right? Of course not – but if it was easy, you wouldn't be impressing management with your decision-making skills.

Once you have decided, however, then you need to record *why* you made this decision. Put together a summary of the information and decision-making process you have used – a memo is the usual form, though you may have signed risk assessments in more formal businesses. This is your basis for communicating (and defending) the decision to management and others who were affected. It's also something you can point to several years down the track, when some idiot has messed up implementation of your idea, to say 'it's not my fault, we planned it correctly at the start'.

Manage the risks, consequences, and communication:

Actually making the decision is rarely the end of your problems. Every major decision will have a host of follow-on outcomes and decisions which flow from it, and each of these will need to be managed. You will also have to communicate the decision and consequences to everyone involved, which may in turn require you to manage any impacted relationships.

To do this, you need to actually identify the consequences before you make the decision. Here are a few questions which you should ask yourself:

- Which relationships may be affected (be they business or personal)?
- What actions are required to implement this option?
- What actions are required to transition from the old processes to the new?
- Do I have to make other decisions to bring this option to conclusion?
- Does it impact previously-made decisions? And if so, do I need to change any of my previous decisions?
- Who needs to know about this decision?

You will also need to implement risk-mitigation measures for all of the risks which were identified in the previous steps. This may include monitoring (following certain parameters which would indicate that a risk is about to occur), preventative actions (designed to stop a certain risk from occurring), accelerative actions (which bring wanted opportunities faster to fruition), and pre-defined conditional actions (check-points where you will take a certain action based on the situation at the time).

And lastly, but certainly not least, you need to communicate this to everyone else. You should have identified all the relevant stakeholders during the earlier steps, and this list will be used to create the communication plan – who finds out what, and when. Getting this right is vital to implementing any new process – communication makes people feel involved, which reduces their natural unhappiness with change and avoids much of the resistance to the new approach.

It's often best to take a three-stage (or more) approach to communicating the outcome of a decision-making process. Those who are more closely invested in the outcome should be informed first – preferably via direct phone call or chat (they will appreciate the personal touch, and you have the chance to smooth over any problems in private, before it blows up into a bigger drama). Then you spread the outcome to a wider group who will be affected, but to a lesser extent – this can be done via a series of meetings. Finally there are those who are kind of involved, but they don't really care – this is where the email announcement comes in.

Regardless of who you are communicating to, it's important to provide both the outcome and a justification for the decision. This does not have to be the *real* justification, but it should be something that your audience can latch onto. A believable justification makes everyone feel better about the upcoming changes and minimises the feeling of being forced into an outcome they don't want.

Persuading others that you've made the right decision

As we've mentioned above, communicating the outcome of any decision is often more important than actually making the decision. You'll have to persuade many other people, from peers to managers to your team, that you know what you are doing, and that you've made the right choice. That's where the additional information in this section comes in.

Who do you need to persuade?

The first question to ask is quite simple – who do you need to persuade that your idea is a good one? The list starts at the most important person for your career (your manager) and progresses downwards to the peripherally involved.

- **Your direct manager**: Your direct manager is the one who has direct veto power over most of your decisions, and the one who will need to defend it to higher management levels. They are also the one who controls your career path, which means it is important to keep them informed and happy. Put a lot of effort into selling your decision to your direct manager, as this is the first and most important gate which you need to get through.

- **Other managers:** There will be other managers involved in any major decision – perhaps higher in the chain than you, perhaps the heads of other departments, perhaps connected in a 'matrix' way. These tend to have a lot of power to block or delay ideas which they don't like, which means that your chosen approach will die quickly if you cannot convince them of its value.
- **Employees affected by the decision**: People directly affected by a decision need to be told what is happening and why, with a targeted effort made to get them involved and supporting the change. Although they (usually) can't *stop* a decision they don't like, there are a million ways to delay or make 'minor mistakes' during implementation, which together will make the project a nightmare.
- **Employees indirectly affected**: These are the people who are not directly involved in the outcome of your decision, but who interact with the affected areas, people, or processes. Those who are slightly affected by a decision should be informed of what is going on, as well as why, but you do not need to put effort into persuading them to the cause. It's happening, and they will need to adapt.
- **The rest**: The rest of the company isn't really affected and probably doesn't really care. You can give them a short summary of what's happening via email, but they can be safely ignored for the remainder of your communication plan.

Planning the communication strategy

Although it seems somewhat overdone, having a communication strategy is a vital part of selling your idea to the rest of the company. You should start out by determining the answers to a few basic questions:

- **What information should be provided?** You are providing information on your decision, but *how much* information do you need to share? It needs to be sufficient detail that those affected will understand your motivations, as this will help them to feel involved in the decision and thus more likely to support you. You should also be able to give a 'future plan' alongside this, a roadmap, however vague, of what will happen next and how long it will take. Note that this does not have to be the real roadmap, nor do you have to explain your real motivations for making a decision – but it should be close enough to the truth or plausible enough that people will accept it.

- **What medium will be the most effective?** There are many different ways to get a message across. You can pass it on in personal chats with individuals or small groups (the best approach when dealing with those directly affected and who can influence your chance of success). You can give a speech to a larger group (for those affected, but whose opinions aren't really that important). Or you can blast information out via group emails and departmental announcements (for those who are merely interested in the outcome). There are many other options – videos, press releases, subtle whispering campaigns orchestrated by colleagues. Which of these is best to use is very dependent on who you are talking to and what information you need to provide.
- **Is my presentation phrased in the right language?** People speak many different languages – not in the sense of 'German' or 'English', but rather the language of their profession and their personal interests. If you are persuading the finance department, then you should focus on cost-saving, increased income, and other financial outcomes. If you speak to HR, talk about employee retention. If you speak to your team, discuss their talents, ability to overcome problems, and the way that this will lead to bonuses and promotion. If you want to persuade, speak to their interests.
- **What negative responses might I receive?** You will never have an important decision which is simply accepted. Someone will always complain, someone will be negatively affected, someone will have championed the other side and will need to be cheered up. This means you need to plan ahead for their complaints, their nasty questions and requests for explanation. Determine the correct answer to these ahead of time, practice it to make sure you can get the answer out without sounding too rehearsed.
- **What questions will come up?** This is the more relaxed version of the previous point. Even those who are in favour of your idea will want to know more – how will it be implemented, what's in it for me, when are we doing it, etc. As above, you should think of the likely questions which will be asked, and come up with an answer to them. If you cannot think of a good answer, then think of a response which will put the question off to later – though be aware that this can be very tricky to do well.
- **When and how will I present?** Lastly comes the logistics side of the discussion. Are you having a meeting with the directly-

impacted? Which meeting room will you book? When will you have it, and when will you meet the next group? Rumours fly almost instantly for important decisions, so you need to have almost simultaneous communication occurring to prevent people from hearing via other means (and when they do, you can be sure that they will be angry about it).

Sell the idea

The planning is done, the people are identified, and you are ready to do the actual persuasion. How you go about this is heavily dependent on the message and audience, but there are a few general rules you should follow:

- **Use clear and specific language**: People are very capable of noticing when others try to hide a lack of information by saying lots and lots of nothing. This is even more apparent as you discuss topics with higher levels of management, who are (generally) hired for their ability to be clever. This means that regardless of who you are talking to, they will notice when you are trying to avoid a question or avoid giving details. Be clear, be specific. Not only is it easier to understand, it helps people believe you and influences them to your side.

- **Put your ideas in a positive, constructive light**: It seems obvious, but it is amazing how many people try to persuade others by underselling their ideas and then saying "but it's the best we have". Be positive, emphasize that this idea will *improve* things rather than simply avoid problems.

- **Emphasise that you will help them adapt**: Most people don't like change, it makes them scared and angry. As most major decisions require a major change of some sort, you will be forced to lead others through a change which they will be suspicious and possibly scared of. You should emphasise that you are there to help them through these difficult times, and that you will put a lot of effort into helping them adapt to the new situation. This reassurance calms people down, which makes the implementation much easier.

- **Ask them what they will do**: This ties into the previous point. By asking people what they will do to incorporate the change, you show that you are empathetic to their problems and want to hear how they will overcome them. It may be that you don't really care, but the mere act of asking give the impression that you *do* care. This in turn will warm others to you, your idea, and the efforts needed to implement it.

8. Interacting with others

Office politics is based on the many different interactions which we have on a daily basis. If you are bad at these interactions, constantly missing the point or making a fool of yourself, then you are going to be bad at office politics as well. This chapter covers the fundamentals of interacting with others, from the basics of communication through to holding discussions on tough and risky topics.

Communication basics

Success in office politics relies on communication – if you want to understand the desires of others (a basic requirement for predicting actions) then you first need to find out what they are. How do you manage this? Quite simple, you talk to them.

Of course, talking is a skill like any other – the more you practice, the more likely you are to do well. There are a few basic rules here which we will cover in more detail within the section:

- Learn how to listen to people
- How you say things is more important than what you say
- Everyone has a reason for their actions, even if it is not immediately apparent
- Building empathy pays off in the long run
- You need to be able to sell things – ideas, projects, or even dreams

Learn how to listen

Very few people are able to listen well – most of us tend to drift off in the middle of a conversation or meeting, we think about what we're making for dinner tonight, did I reply to that email before, why hasn't he realised that shirt is hideous? And so on. Mundane topics and distractions tend to pop into our minds all the time, and this pulls our attention away from the topic at hand.

Which means that those who *can* listen well, who can walk out of meetings knowing what has happened and what they are going to do about it, have a major advantage. Everyone else will rely on the (often inaccurate) meeting minutes to tell them what to do, while the good listener can get things moving straight away. This, as you can imagine, looks good.

So how do you listen well?

- **Concentrate**: Obviously. If you aren't concentrating, then you won't pay attention to the information which is being passed on to you. Focus on the conversation or meeting, ruthlessly ignore distracting thoughts which pop into your head. If it's a distracting but important idea or question, make a note for later and then *ignore it until then*. The meeting is for the meeting topic.
- **Don't think of your next argument**: It's always very tempting to think of the next argument you will use, how you will rebut their last comment, how you have really good evidence supporting your position. Stop it. Although tempting, these thoughts simply distract you from focusing on what your counterpart is saying, which means you will miss vital information as it slips by.
- **Ask questions**: There are three good reasons to ask questions in the meeting. One is that it will force others to explain unclear points to you, helping your understanding. Second is that the act of thinking up questions gets you involved in the meeting, helping your recollection of the topics. And third, in contrast to the silent listeners, people who ask questions are noticed by the rest of the attendees – which means you will gain a reputation as an active, interested participant.
- **Identify the main idea**: Any time someone speaks, they are trying to get a message across. This message can be subtle, it can be obvious, it may even be completely different to what their *words* are saying. But there is a message, a main idea, and you need to identify what this is before acting on what they say.
- **Listen for the rationale**: There is (usually) some sort of rationale behind an idea, a reason as to why you should pay attention to it. The rationale is the first place to look to understand ulterior motives, and the first place to attack if you want to discredit an idea. But you can do neither of these things if you can't find the rationale in the first place.
- **Listen for key words**: Some words are more important than others. A day-long meeting on process optimisation will bore the participants half to death – but the moment someone mentions workforce reduction as a result of these optimisations, suddenly everyone is completely awake. Know what the most important key words for your position are, and be extra alert for these.
- **Watch the non-verbal behaviour**: Most of our communication happens non-verbally, and you will find that body language will

often show something completely different to their words. The way we sit is a simple example of this, leaning back indicates a feeling of confidence, hunching forward or crossed arms shows defensiveness, leaning forward or backward in response to you doing the same indicates interest in you and your information. You need to be careful here, of course, as it is easy to over-interpret the actions of others. Always keep the context in mind.

- **Watch the use of props**: It's often difficult to know what hands should be doing during a conversation, and so many take to holding something. This prop extends the space a person takes up, which in turn makes them feel confident. It is also possible to use this to your advantage – grand gestures with a pen or pointer will make you seem more important, providing others with a coffee before giving bad news lets them 'hide' behind the cup. It is, obviously, a minor thing, but it adds up.
- **Summarise**: Take what you have heard so far and summarise it to the others. Add a comment that this is your understanding and ask if it is correct. Not only will it encourage further communication and clarification, but it allows you to subtly modify the discussion in your preferred direction.
- **Organise in your mind**: Don't just sit there and let the conversation flow over you. Analyse what people are saying, mentally question their motives, ask yourself if this all makes sense. Think of what the likely outcome of the discussion will be, and what is best for you.
- **Organise on paper**: All the thinking in the previous point is exhausting, and you will find that you forget the ever-so-important idea within a minute, as the next pile of information comes through. So write it down. Take notes, in paper or electronic format. Don't assume that you'll remember it, because you won't. Perhaps you'll remember after the meeting – but you will have a tonne of unread emails waiting when you get back to your desk, a couple of conversations on the way, and by then the memory is gone.

How you say it is more important than what you say

We spend a lot of our time worrying about what we are going to say. But we rarely think about the fact that *how* we say things has a far greater impact on others than *what* we say. Enthusiastic, happy people will bring a mirroring

Interacting with others

emotion out in those they speak to – often in an unconscious reaction – and this applies for other emotions which we express in our voice as well.

For those who are trying to develop their careers and communication skills, there are three 'voices' which will bring them a long way towards success. These are the positive voice, the in-control voice, and the assertive voice.

- The **positive voice** is light and encouraging, the tone an easy-going and good-natured person would take. Make sure you relax and smile while talking, it will come across even when speaking over the phone. This tone encourages collaboration and new ideas, and it should be your default for most interactions in the workplace.
- The **in-control voice** is slower, pitched deeper, and has a downward inflection at the end of each sentence. Upwards inflection signifies a question, those who habitually do this for all sentences give the impression of uncertainty and a lack of power. Speak clearly and slowly, do not give the impression that you are unsure of anything. This voice says that you are confident and competent, and that you are here to solve a problem.
- The **assertive voice** is a clear signal that you are the more important one in the discussion, and that the other person *will* do what you are telling them to do. You do not inflect upwards, you speak entirely seriously, and there is no hint of uncertainty or asking in your tone. It is very dangerous to use, as you will often trigger a push-back from your counterpart (either obviously or passive-aggressively). But when it does work, you can save a lot of discussion and negotiation by simply cutting through to what will be done.

Correctly using these three voices is a key method for getting your point across. Use the positive voice as much as you can in general conversation, as it will open up others to you as a person and, by extension, your ideas. Switch to the in-control version when things are looking dramatic and there is some sort of crisis in the making. And if you truly reach the point where you have to tell people exactly what to do, no ifs or buts, then use the assertive voice.

Beyond this you should always try to follow the main rules of speaking. Vary your tone and your volume, to avoid sounding monotonous – boring people may be competent, but they are rarely liked. Try to shift your voice to a lower range (without sounding ridiculous), as we are subconsciously primed to accept deeper voices as more reliable. And use silence judiciously, as a pause to emphasise an idea or to encourage your counterpart to speak up.

Everyone has, and needs, a reason

One of the strange things about human behaviour is that we are always looking for the reason behind events. This is a good thing in many ways (science is based on the idea after all), but at the same time it leaves us likely to over-value ideas which come with a nice story or justification attached.

- **Always include a reason for your request**: You can make any number of stupid requests to other people, *as long as you give a reason for asking*. Even more usefully, this reason doesn't need to be a good one – it can be arbitrary or even a complete lie, the important thing is that there is something for the listener to latch on to and think 'this is why I should say yes'. This means that any time you ask for help, a favour, etc., you should follow it up with a 'because'. Try it out, you will find it surprisingly effective.

- **Ask for favours**: Another way to use this is to imply the existence of a reason through the words we choose. An example here is starting your message with "can you do me a favour?" This automatically implies the rest of the sentence ("because I will then owe you a favour"), which in turn lights up the idea of reciprocity in your counterparts' head. Reciprocity is a powerful glue in social cohesion, and thus even a simple sentence like this is surprisingly effective at getting others to do things that they don't particularly want to do. Of course, it is up to you whether you return the 'owed' favour or not, but this is a decision for a later moment.

- **Insinuate reasons for their behaviour**: Sometimes projects need input from your theoretical sponsor in upper management, yet every email you send disappears into a crowded inbox, never to be heard from again. A simple trick – write once again, mention the lack of communication on the project, and then add "I can only assume your priorities have changed". Note that you will follow suit and deprioritise the project from date X, at least 1-2 weeks away. By implying that they have a reason to stop the project, you trigger a feeling of worry and denial in their minds. You will inevitably find a hurried and apologetic response on the next day.

Now all of this is fine, but in the daily organisational life you will often feel that other people are acting irrationally. Sometimes this is the case, there are crazy people all over the place. But more often than not they are simply basing their decision on different information to that which is available to you. Irrational activity is usually a sign that there is more going on, and that you need to figure out *why* they are being irrational.

In general, there are three main reasons why someone will be acting oddly (assuming that they aren't crazy, of course):

- **They aren't fully informed**: They are missing some important piece of information which, if they had it, would cause them to act differently. In these cases, you need to figure out what they don't know, and (tactfully) provide it to them.
- **They have underlying constraints**: There is something preventing them from acting in a particular way, (legal advice, personal beliefs, fear of having a mistake found out, they are being blackmailed) and this constraint is not known to you. Here you need to determine the constraint and figure out a way around it.
- **They have hidden interests**: Everyone has their own goals and desires, and these will often conflict with the goals or desires of their job or position (for example, short-term success in a role is good for your promotion, even if you achieve it in ways which are bad for the company long-term). If you are seeing odd behaviour from a counterpart, it's quite possible that they are acting in a way which is completely rational – but *only* if you know what their hidden interest is.

Once you have a reasonable idea of what is causing their particular behaviour, then you can begin to look for ways to solve it. This could involve providing extra information or simply clever bargaining to trade something you can provide for something they want.

The fourth possibility is that they are simply irrational, crazy, or sociopathic. This is unfortunately much more common in the business world than we would prefer, and often leads to situations where your best response is to bypass or minimise their involvement. Whether this comes in the form of finding alternative collaborators, going above their head, or simply getting them fired is a dependent on your exact circumstances.

Building empathy
It's important not to misunderstand this point. Being empathetic is not about sitting at home crying to soap operas and the beauty of roses. Being

empathetic is about understanding others, their underlying motivations, their positions on issues, and how they communicate.

It certainly doesn't mean that you will help them achieve their goals, or that you won't trash their career to improve your chances. But it does mean that you need to think about who you are dealing with, and understand who they are. If nothing else, understanding someone makes it easier to guide their actions.

Beyond this, managers who demonstrate empathy have been shown to have better results from their teams, particularly in cultures which emphasise concentration of power and fixed 'layers' of importance in society. These 'high power distance' cultures (the typical example here is Japan) focus on power as providing stability, and there is a built-in expectation that those higher in the chain will protect those below them.

Empathy, of course, takes work – you can't just roll on in, pretend that you care, and have people gushing about your amazing empathetic skills a week later. It is difficult to figure out what people want, it is effort to get into the specifics of their problem. And you'll probably be quite bad at it to start with, so

So how do you build an empathetic demeanour?

- **Listen**: Listen more than you talk. Try to follow active listening, the art of focusing on your conversational partner, taking what they say, summarising it back to them, and using this to develop further questions about the topic. In essence, you aren't just listening to what they say, you are talking to them about it.
- **Learn how to ask questions**: If someone is coming to you with an issue, they must think it is important. Even if you can't understand it yourself. Which is why you need to ask questions to get to the root of the matter – try to find out the specifics of the problem, why it is important to them, who else might be involved, and what they would consider a successful resolution. Ask specific questions, don't waste time on general ones.
- **Understand their priorities and problems**: It is hard to understand what other people are doing, particularly in the workplace when they are responsible for different projects or even in completely different departments. This disconnect will inevitably be a problem when the next crisis pops up, so take the time to solve

it beforehand. Go find that expert, have a chat, ask really basic questions about what they do, try to find out what happens in a typical day. This sort of basic knowledge will help you understand what they consider important, which in turn helps you to negotiate later on.

- **Watch for signs of overwork**: As a manager, one of the easiest ways to show empathy is to watch for signs of overwork, then offer to reduce the workload. Or, if this isn't possible, describe why the workload is so bad and what plans you have to the future which will improve it.
- **Be interested in hopes and goals**: Your team and your colleagues will have their own hopes and aspirations, areas in which they want to develop and goals they wish to achieve. Take an interest in these, use your talents and connections to help them succeed. This will not only gain you the reputation of an empathetic colleague, but will strengthen your network throughout the business.
- **You are dealing with people**: This can be hard to remember sometimes, given the high-stress corporate world we live in. So try to consciously treat others as people, not just co-workers. Chat for a bit, ask about their home life, share personal details. Be willing to help out when they have personal problems, be compassionate when they talk about personal loss. All of this builds rapport and helps gain trust.
- **Don't assume the worst**: If something happens, it's usually a result of forgetfulness rather than incompetence, and more likely incompetence than malice. Give people the benefit of the doubt. Unless it turns into a pattern, then you should start making plans to have them removed or neutralised.
- **Be open**: Don't prejudge people, don't shut them down if their ideas or experiences clash with yours. Be open, ask questions, and see what they think.

On the other hand, sometimes you cannot develop an understanding of the other person. Perhaps there is a rush to get things done, perhaps they are actively hostile to your advances, perhaps you can't be bothered putting the effort in. One way to short-cut the development of empathy involves guessing the emotions another is feeling, giving it an explicit label, and repeating it back to them.

How does this work?

- **Guess their emotions**: This is something you can usually discern from their words, tone, and associated body language. Watch for their small reactions to different topics, look at the situation you are both in and extrapolate how you would feel.
- **Label it**: Guessed an emotion? Repeat it back to them, prefacing it with a phrase such as 'it sounds like…' or 'it looks like…' (e.g. "it looks like you are stressed about the project"). Using 'it looks' rather than 'I feel' makes it a neutral statement and avoids any focus on yourself – it also lets you backpedal if they disagree completely.
- **Wait**: Now don't say anything. Wait for them to agree with you, or disagree, and provide additional information on their current emotional state.
- **Repeat**: This is a conversation, oddly enough, which means it will be several cycles of discussion, labelling emotion, building rapport, and the like. Over time, you will build up an emotional connection faster than you otherwise would, which in turn helps build the relationship.

Use this method to bring underlying emotions to the surface, where they can be acknowledged and either reinforced or neutralised. In general you should focus on clearing away negative emotions first, as the reasons why they *won't* deal with you are more important than the reasons why they *will*.

If there is an underlying *negative* emotion, then you should label it consciously, without offering judgement. It often helps to think up every possible fear or accusation they could point at you (e.g. "you're only doing this to make your bonus"), and then deliberately list them at the very start of the conversation. Saying it out loud makes it appear exaggerated, which in turn encourages your counterpart to downplay them in their mind.

Know how to sell things

One of the most important skills that anyone climbing the ladder needs is the ability to *sell* things. This isn't just selling products (though this is a great way to get rich if you're good enough), it's also selling your ideas, selling your value, even selling the value of your team. No matter how clever you are, if you can't persuade others that you are solving their problems, then you're going to fail.

So how do you sell thing? This is a massive topic and one which we can't cover in detail here. But here are a few important things to remember:

- **Solve a real problem**: Selling isn't about what you are offering, selling is about what the other person needs. You have to identify what they are looking for, what their need is – whether it be real or imaginary. Then you show how your offer will solve that need. Don't lose track of this, make sure you focus like a laser on how you can solve their problem, and you'll be set.
- **Ask questions**: This ties in clearly with the previous point. You can't know what people need until you ask them, so ask them. Don't start pitching your amazing idea until you're clear on what they need, or you'll pitch the wrong thing and screw up your entire chance.
- **Keep them talking**: People love talking about themselves. Encourage that. It makes them like you more, gives you information on what they need, and lets you gently direct towards the fantastic solution which you are offering. Avoid giving advice, telling them about yourself, or just talking too much.
- **Don't 'check in', include something of value with your reminder**: Yes, you should be keeping in contact with people you are selling to. No, you shouldn't just 'check in' via voicemail or send a 'touch base' email. No-one reads your email, they delete your message, they don't care and they won't remember. So bribe them with something they do want – include links to interesting articles, drop some info they might not know, bribe them with donuts when coming. People are greedy, and they like getting stuff. Tap into that greed to improve their opinion of you.
- **Don't be a loser**: Be confident, don't spend your time trying to follow them around begging for the sale. Neediness looks pathetic, and it will either scare them away or invite their contempt. In love or business, never be needy.
- **Offer fewer choices**: Too many options leads to paralysis, as you spend your time trying to decide which of these many options is the best. Make things simple – offer an expensive option, a cheap option, and a mid-range option. Most people will go for the middle, so price it accordingly.
- **Make clients, not just sales**: Regardless of what you're selling, you need to create a relationship with the person buying. Ask questions, chat, try to find out what exactly they need and how you can meet that need. In the end, we all prefer to give our business to people we like – which is why you want to be the one they like.

- **Smile, laugh**: Not in the sense of 'live laugh love' or any other inspirational rubbish, but go out there and smile at people, then make them laugh. People smile back, people laugh with you. And this builds a connection which you can use to sell your solution.

Interacting with your colleagues

The way you interact with your colleagues should be tailored to their position with respect to you. The jokes and conversations you hold with your closest colleagues will not be appropriate to have with subordinates, and trying to do so will only diminish your reputation and powerbase. There are several levels of interaction partner, as described in the following sections.

Interacting with your closest associates

You will inevitably have a close circle of colleagues in your team, the ones whose opinions you respect, and whom you depend on to get things done. These are the main drivers of your eventual success, and so you need to be sure that you are communicating well. Never assume that they remember what you've agreed on or what they are expecting in return.

Some useful rules when dealing with your closest associates are as follows:

- **Communicate**: Always keep people informed regarding what is occurring and why. Something which seems unimportant to you may be extremely important for them, and acting without agreement or discussion can lead to anger and arguments.
- **Don't play them against each other**: Although it sounds fun, don't try to play power games by setting one of your associates against another.
- **Choose wisely**: You need to have a good team of people supporting you. Choose your closest associates based on the following strengths – diligence, accuracy, efficiency in running their area, ability to lead their teams, ability to fit into the team, and ability to be ambitious *without* being devious. Base your decisions on their past performance – few people change their behaviour all that much over time.
- **Show respect**: Treat them well, ask their opinions, and provide criticism in the way which you would like to receive it. If problems are coming up (either from outside or within your own team) then face it openly and discuss it within the group.

Interacting with others

- **Assign clear lanes**: When assigning tasks and responsibilities, make sure that there is no overlap between the work each associate will do. Employees need their own projects, and the feeling that they 'own' something – don't be so vague with delegation that they fight over responsibility.
- **Actually delegate**: Once you've delegated a task, you need to allow that person to make decisions, even if you would do it in a different way. Don't be a micromanager.
- **Avoid the evil vizier problem**: In every fairy tale, the second-in-command to the king or sultan is evil and merely waiting until they can steal the throne. Avoid designating a single person as the obvious second-in-charge for your team, as this creates a clear temptation for them to become the evil vizier. Instead, try to split responsibility amongst two or more people, or choose one person who is close to retirement in any case.
- **Allow criticism, but only in private**: Criticism and discussion of your ideas by the inner circle is absolutely welcome, it helps perfect your approach. But this criticism should be done in private, behind closed doors – people who speak badly of you and your ideas in public generally should not keep their jobs for long.

Interacting with your equals

In any large organisation, you'll have a number of people who are at an equal 'rank' to you in the hierarchy. They may head groups with greater or less importance, but this is irrelevant – the important thing is to consider all of them potential allies in reaching your goals. The best way to do this is to make it clear that you *are* equals, and that you all have the overall success of the company at heart.

How does this work? Here are a few suggestions:

- **Focus on the larger organisation**: In any meeting with other equals, you are there to represent your team or departments interests. But you are also there for the overall success of the organisation, and you need to keep this in mind while arguing your case. Sometimes you will have to accept a 'bad' outcome for your group in order to achieve an overall win – and the others will realise this and respect you more for it.
- **Prepare beforehand**: You should know what you are talking about, which means you need to prepare for any important meeting

beforehand. Make sure you have all the facts and information in place, make sure you can argue the merits of your ideas. Discuss your ideas with potential opponents or supporters before the meeting to bring them to your side.

- **Don't try to dominate the meeting**: Everyone is an equal, and they will absolutely resent your conscious attempt to act as the leader. Don't try to dominate the others, simply *show* that you are more knowledgeable and are a better leader than they are – they will follow along.
- **Make friends**: Making close friends with subordinates is rarely a good idea, but you should take the opportunity to befriend your equals. The regular, open discussions helps you grow as a leader, while forming a stronger political alliance within the organisation. These friendships will also stay throughout your career, making a valuable part of your network

Interacting with your subordinates

If you are a manager, then your eventual success is based on the success of your team members. Certainly you are responsible for guiding and managing them, but they need to be competent and successful in their own tasks on their own terms. Which means that one of your main jobs is to smooth their paths out so that they can do their jobs, provide the inspiration and pride that they need to do it, and help them celebrate when they succeed.

A successful leader needs to create a sense of pride within the group, a feeling that they can accomplish anything, solve any problem. And they need to do this by clearly and visibly leading – by being there for their people.

There are a few simple rules of thumb to follow here.

- **Be visible**: Your team needs to see that you are there. Wander through the offices, say hi to employees at their desks, stand up the front in group meetings and make it clear that you are managing the team.
- **Back your team up**: You are your teams' representative to the wider organisation, and part of that is supporting their interests. Why should they do their best work for you, if you won't defend them when needed?

- **Be approachable**: You need to be willing to talk about issues – and this willingness needs to be clear to your team as well. Talk to your team, have an inbox where people can drop off their ideas, actively seek out feedback on how things are going. You will get a wide variety of feedback, some of it silly, but you should follow everything up and handle it respectfully.
- **Be clear when delegating**: Give clear goals when delegating tasks to your team members, if a particular approach needs to be followed then make this clear. Do not dump your responsibility onto them, if you should make a decision, then make it.
- **Explain your plans**: You should always explain as much of your plan as possible to your subordinates. Explain why you are doing something, what the eventual goal is. This builds trust for those inevitable times when you cannot explain why you are doing something – your team will follow you based on the trust you have built up before.
- **Support decisions from higher up**: Regardless of the problems you have with a decision or mandate from higher management, you should support that decision in public with your team members. One of your main roles is to pass information up and down the chain of command, and this includes unwelcome information. If nothing else, make sure you support these decisions because you are likely to lose your job if you don't.

Getting your ideas across

You are undoubtedly clever and have many brilliant ideas which could bring success and riches to the organisation or company. Yet no-one listens to, or takes the time to understand just how brilliant these ideas are. Why are you surrounded by people who cannot see the obvious solution?

Sounds familiar? This is a common complaint for many employees. Unfortunately, the solution for this problem has to come from your end – it is not their fault that they cannot understand, it is *your fault* that you haven't explained it enough.

What do we mean? The way in which you communicate ideas is vital to getting these ideas accepted, taken up and implemented. Here are a few brief hints, with further detail on the importance of stories coming in below:

- **One idea at a time**: You can't jump randomly from idea to idea and expect your audience to follow you. Focus on one idea or topic at a time, make sure they understand what you mean, and then smoothly move on to your next idea.
- **Get buy-in of each idea**: Just as you should focus on one idea at a time, you should make sure that everyone accepts your idea before you move onto the next one. This doesn't mean they have to agree, simply that they can follow the logic. This helps you string ideas together in a chain to persuade them of your overall aim.
- **Simple, brief**: People get bored easily. Long emails, long discussions, complicated words, all of these things will cause others to tune out. Keep everyone hanging on your ideas by expressing them in a simple, brief way.
- **Personalise your message**: As we've said, people get bored easily. Improve your chances of them paying attention by changing your message to focus on their needs and interests.
- **Watch your tone and body language**: Words are kind of irrelevant when it comes to communication, most of your message comes from the *way* you say things – your tone and the body language attached to them.
- **Respond to emotions, not words**: As for you, so for them – what they say is not as important as how they say it. Watch for cues showing your conversational partners emotional state, this will tell you what they really think of your ideas, and thus how to overcome it.
- **Listen to their responses**: No-one likes to feel railroaded into an action, no-one wants to find themselves in a one-sided conversation. Give them time to talk, listen to what they are saying. This is free information which you can use to target your message even further – why waste the opportunity?

Selling ideas through stories

Deep down, we're suckers for a good story. This is why the most successful professionals are usually the ones which have mastered the art of telling a story – of describing their vision and goals in a way that makes the listener think 'wow'. This is a difficult skill to master – you need to talk about your successes in a way which is impressive, engaging, but not boastful, and use this to draw others into your schemes. Nor is this limited to the top CEOs, everyone who has to communicate with others can benefit from wrapping their ideas in the form of a narrative.

The world is full of data and information. If you are in a typical office job, then you are probably responsible for or involved in analysing data in some way. This can be as exotic as pharmaceutical clinical trial results or as mundane as the office coffee machine refills – the important thing is that there is data, you have to interpret this data, and that this interpretation is needed to make some sort of decision.

But people who make decisions tend to have many other things trying to catch their attention, which means that you need to distil the vast pile of information down to a couple of main points. Then you need to provide your recommendation in a clear and engaging way.

It's important to remember that data visualisation (the pretty graphs you make) is not the same as telling a story. They relate to each other, sure, but although many programs exist to help make nice graphics, the art of storytelling is up to you.

There are a few simple points which you should keep in mind when crafting your story:

- **Find the narrative**: Look at your data and conclusions – have you got a story to tell here? A surprising hook, a captivating purpose or idea? If yes, you should damn well tell that story, don't waste the audiences' time.
- **Know your audience**: Who are your audience? What background information do they need to know in order to understand your ideas? Are they newbies – getting their first exposure to your subject but not wanting oversimplification? Generalists who have heard of the topic but want a better overview? Managers who are looking for actions they can take based on your data? Experts – who want the details and none of this storytelling rubbish? Or executive-level leaders, who only want the summary? Target your presentation to their needs.
- **Provide context**: How do your recommendations fit into the wider world? Decision-makers need to match your ideas with the wider business, which means they will want some sort of context in any case. Provide your own to make your ideas more persuasive.

- **Be objective**: It's easy to make a piece of data say anything you want – you can fiddle with graph layouts, pick your favourite analysis or stats, choosing sneaky colour schemes. In the short term this is very effective, and you can push decisions in your chosen direction quite easily. But soon people will start to *think* about your message, and then they will realise what you're doing. It's even quicker when dealing with an intelligent or expert audience.
- **Linear timelines**: Flashbacks and *in media res* is fine for novels, but not for a business presentation. Stick to a linear approach – provide the background, discuss the findings, present the implications. Don't assume that your audience can follow you through all of your mental leaps, guide them to the final solution.
- **Bring in emotion**: You'll have the best impact when you get emotional investment from your audience, particularly if that is focused on a single concept. How do you do this? Tell a personal story or develop a fake persona who is impacted by the event and recommendation. This sounds wishy-washy, but has been shown to improve recall of the idea and leads to better acceptance of proposals.
- **Frame the presentation according to the audience**: This goes along with knowing your audience. Figure out who they will be, and how they would normally see the world. Then adjust your approach to match their expectations of what a 'recommendation' should look like.

Saying no to others

When you get right down to it, the only person who truly has your best interests at heart is you. Everyone wants something different, and sometimes their desires will line up with yours. That's great, it makes things easy. But sometimes you'll be asked to do things which aren't in your best interest – to take on additional and thankless work, to lead a project which is bound to fail, to move to some godforsaken corner of Alaska to help provide 'much needed leadership'. And this is where you need to say 'no'.

Saying no to equals

Saying 'no' is hard. You'll be very, very tempted to cave in and say 'yes' to the request. You'll have pressure from colleagues, guilt trips from management, people asking why you don't just go along. It can't be that much extra effort, right?

Interacting with others

Fuck them. If you are certain that this is not in your best interest, then you need to step up and push back. It's your career, after all, and while managers *like* a pushover, they *promote* one who can keep their priorities under pressure.

This doesn't mean you should be rude. There is a fine art to saying 'no' subtly yet firmly, even convincing your colleague that it was their idea in the first place. This means you shouldn't say 'no' explicitly, you should always hide it in a way which appears to be polite and helpful. If you work at it, you can say no several times before you really have to cut them off:

- **By pausing:** Once the request comes in, just pause. Say nothing for about three seconds, enough to make it slightly uncomfortable. Then ask what they mean. Socially astute people will pick up the hint at this point, the others will require further work.
- **By asking for help**: "How am I going to do that?" Force them to think about the downsides by asking for help on how to implement their silly idea (we go over this in more detail in the next section)
- **By asking for prioritisation**: Note that you have multiple projects ongoing, which you cannot completely fulfil. If there is something else you are doing for your colleague, ask if they want you to deprioritise that task in favour of the new one.
- **By praising their generosity**: "I'm sorry. That's a tempting offer, but it just doesn't work for me". Make them feel better about offering you something, but make it clear that it's not enough for you to take the deal.
- **By showing regret**: "I'm sorry, but I just can't do that." You're more direct, and you trigger a little bit of empathy for your inability to help them out.
- **By saying no**: "I'm sorry, no." Polite, delivered gently to keep them on your side, and clear enough to get the point across to everyone.

Saying no to managers

These approaches are perfectly valid when saying 'no' to people who are roughly at your level in the organisation. Unfortunately actively saying no to your direct manager is a significantly more difficult task, and one where you will have to be a little bit clever.

For all that we hear of 'collaborative environments' and the like, there are an awful lot of top-down, hierarchy-centred managers out there. Those who will tell you what to do, and will happily resort to intimidation or shouting to get their way. Outright arguing with these people is rarely a good idea, you will end up angry and stressed, there will be shouting in the office and political fallout for months afterwards. Instead, you should let them think of reasons why their idea won't work.

How do you do this?

- **Use the 'in control' voice**: Speak calmly and slowly, in a manner that shows you are both competent and capable of solving their current problem. This reassures them that you want to help, not simply reject their idea.
- **Always say "I'm sorry"**: Start off with an apology. Your intention is to request more information, because you are terribly interested in solving their problem. Apologising at the start reassures them that you are not rejecting their idea, you just want help understanding.
- **Mirror their last few words**: Repeat the last few words in a questioning tone, which will implicitly ask them for more details. Try to mirror in such a way that you ask for detail on part of their request which is implicitly unreasonable or badly-thought-out.
- **Wait a few seconds**: As they think slightly more about what they are saying, and how this will be implemented in reality.
- **Ask for help with implementation**: Calmly reply: "I'd love to help, but how am I supposed to do that?" Use this moment to point out any challenges in implementation.
- **Repeat**: One round is never enough to kill a stupid idea. But if you keep asking for assistance in a respectful tone, then they will eventually realise the problem on their own.

This works in several ways. First, it *sounds* like you are interested in their project, thus you avoid the nasty argument which occurs when you tell them how stupid their idea is. Secondly it forces attention onto the problems which you need to solve – this not only makes *your* problems *their* problems, but will draw attention to *why* the problems exist. In other words, it gets them onto your side of the discussion, often without even realising it.

Others saying no to you

For all that we talk about saying 'no' to requests you don't like, you will also have to deal with other people saying no to your requests as well. This is a very natural reaction to requests which people aren't too happy about, and it is an almost essential response in a world of irritating people pressuring us to do (or buy) things. Being able to say 'no' is thus a very important requirement for all of us, which is why we instinctively push back against pre-planned speeches which try to railroad us into saying 'yes' to a request.

Luckily for you, this means that a 'no' is very often not a final rejection, it often means 'I am not quite ready to agree', 'I want something else', 'I need more information', or even 'I need time to think it over and discuss with others'. And this is great, because it means they are at least slightly engaged in talking to you (far worse is when people say 'yes' with no intention of helping you, just to get you to go away). You can now probe to find out what their no *really* means, and work on answering that worry.

Simply being able to say no often makes people feel more secure in their positon, and thus more willing to hear your arguments. You can take advantage of this by asking a leading question at the start which will trigger a 'no' from their side, then using this security as a basis for your negotiation. Remember that each 'no' you hear is simply another point where you need to be convincing – after all, they will only *really* agree if they are convinced that your suggestion is aligned with their requirements.

When are they really saying yes?

People will often use a yes to get you to go away, saying 'yes' to shut down the conversation or negotiation and then simply going back on their decision at a later date. This is something you should avoid doing yourself (as people just get irritated), but you are likely to run into it during your office career.

So how do you know that they *really* agree, rather than want you to leave them alone? Generally someone who is willing to agree with you several times, to questions which are phrased slightly differently each time, is actually agreeing. The classic number is three times (from a practical and biblical point of view), but you can push it a bit further if you need the reassurance. Once they agree the first time, make a summary of your aligned way forward and ask if that's correct – that's the second 'yes'. Then ask about success criteria for your implementation, something like "what do we do if we go off track?" This is a third 'yes'.

If you spot inconsistencies or strange body language during this point, it's a potential sign that they aren't really committed to your idea. You can then follow up on problems and provide more persuasion/ideas as necessary.

Getting past 'no'

A firm 'no' can be a challenge for your plans, but it is very rarely a complete deal-breaker. As sales representatives have known for decades, you have to work your way through numerous 'no's before you can finally close the deal with a 'yes'.

Here are a few basic tips for getting past the initial no, and allowing yourself to move into the more useful bargaining phase.

- **Focus on positive outcomes**: Constantly hearing people say no starts to wear on you after a while. Thus it is important that you focus on (and believe in) the idea of getting positive results, even in a gloomy and negative situation.
- **Don't take it personally**: Get your ego out of the way, and accept that you will have many rejections before you have some success.
- **Watch for the 'fake no'**: Rejecting an idea or suggestion is often an instinctive reaction, particularly when your counterpart feels threatened or insecure. They then feel trapped into this response and will hold to it despite further information. When this happens, you need to acknowledge but not accept their response – keep probing to try and find the real reason for their refusal.
- **Counter requests for more information**: Asking for more information (preferably time-consuming data) is a time-honoured way to deflect a proposal without explicitly refusing. If this happens, agree to provide it but ask *specifically* what information they need and then what the follow-up process will be. Never agree to just leave without fixing a plan for later.
- **Counter budget/priority arguments**: If they claim that there is no budget available or that such an idea is outside of the current priorities, then you need to ask what the priorities or budget currently are. Ask probing questions – what are they? How would they be affected by your idea and its amazing benefits? What if budget wasn't an issue? What other problems do they have that you could help with?
- **Passing responsibility**: A particular problem in large organisations, there is always someone else who can be referred to

as the main decision-maker for the project. If they defer to someone else who has authority, then you need to ask who that person is, how you can get to see them, and whether they have any tips for interacting with them. Feel free to ask for hints as they will see this as a compliment – your counterpart is important enough to know the decision-maker, what a feeling.

This is unfortunately not an easy process (if it were, sales reps would not be so well paid). But with time, persistence, and practice, it is possible to become reasonably talented at getting past the initial rejection. After this you are into the world of influencing (page 155) and negotiation (page 171).

Tough Discussions

At some point in your career you will need to have a 'tough' conversation, one which is not particularly fun or pleasant, but which has to be done in order to progress your goals, get your point across, or simply avoid a major problem which is in the making. These are tough and they are *important*, meaning that you can't just hide your head in the sand and hope the issue goes away. But it also means that you have to be clever about how you get involved, because few things make an issue worse than screwing up a 'serious' conversation.

Luckily for you, this section has a heap of details on how to hold a tough conversation, get your meaning across, and avoid making everything worse in the process.

Don't waste time on the 'wrong' conversation

If you're going to put the effort in, then you should obviously be talking about the right thing. And many people get into these discussions and then go wildly off-track, talking about things which aren't relevant or dredging up old complaints.

How do you know if you're talking about the 'wrong' thing? Pretty easy. If you start to get angry or frustrated, if emotions start to rise, then you're probably heading the same way. If you realise that you're heading down a well-worn track into a conversation *which you've had before*, then you are definitely talking about the wrong thing. In these cases the problem is not your partner, it's you. Because you're wasting time talking about the wrong thing.

So what's the right thing to discuss? This is very dependent on the situation, but you can think of it as being three different layers.

- Current difficulty: What event is happening right now and causing you problems?
- Repeating difficulties: What event has happened before and is constantly repeating itself?
- Persistent difficulties: What issue is causing problems between you and the other, be it a lack of trust, complacence, or respect?

These increase in importance, and you need to be careful not to waste time discussing a low level (such as what's going on right now) when the problem is occurring at a higher level (because there's a long-term lack of trust between you). This often means you'll need to discuss a few issues together, or go beyond the problem of the current moment. Don't worry about this. First decide *what* you're going to talk about, *then* figure out how to do it.

Why do you care?

The motives you have matter, because that's what drives your desires, aims, and actions. Which means that you need to figure out why you actually care about any particular topic before you go in and start arguing about it. Obviously you give a damn in one way or another – otherwise you wouldn't be bothering to talk to them.

Generally any motive can be thought of as selfish or community-driven. A selfish motive is about you – you want to win, you want to be right, you want that sports car, you may even just want to avoid conflict. These are the most common motives and the easiest to understand. The community motive is one which is aspirational (creating the best sales group in the region) or inclusive (getting poor kids off the streets). They are big ideas which have long-term goals, which means you'll feel more flexibility about how you achieve them.

Your motives, and how other people *perceive* your motives, are incredibly important in getting your desires across to others. Before you have any important discussion, you should get a clear answer on the following questions:

- What does it *look like* I want, from an outsiders' perspective?
- What do I *really* want? For me, for others, for the group?
- How would I behave if I really wanted *those results*?

Got that figured out? Once you know what you want, you can figure out what other people want as well.

Why do they care?

Tough question to answer, right? And realistically you'll never really be able to know what other people are thinking or why they are so passionate about the issues. What you can do, however, is take a best guess at what a reasonable person thinks and go from there.

I say 'reasonable' here because we generally don't think of others as reasonable. Especially when emotions start to rise, we tend to tell ourselves stories about what the other is thinking – that they're doing this just to screw with you, that they hate you, that everything is a grand plan to get you fired. Worse, this is a spiral – you see something, tell yourself a blatantly-stupid-but-somehow-believable story, get angry about that story, act angry, and then interpret their reaction to your anger with yet another story. A few minutes later you're both screaming at each other and any hope of getting your plan across is gone.

So the core message here is 'don't over-interpret'. Learn to separate the facts of the situation (i.e. what you have absolutely, concretely observed) from your *interpretation* of the facts (the story you tell yourself about their meaning and motive). In particular, you should include your own role in the story which they are telling themselves.

What does this mean? Here's a simple process:

- Determine the *objective* facts surrounding the issue
- Identify where you are interpreting these facts according to your own beliefs
- Determine how others would interpret *your own* actions, e.g.
    o What am I pretending not to notice regarding my role in this problem?
    o Why would a reasonable, decent person do what I am doing? Or what they are doing?
- What should I do right now to move the situation towards my desired goal?

Once you have this down, it's time to communicate.

Communicate your thoughts

Your meaning may be perfectly clear in your head, but that doesn't help your counterpart at all. You need to communicate your thoughts, get your meaning and ideas across, and do so without massively insulting them or causing a fight to start.

How do you do this? It's actually fairly simple:

- First, state the pure facts which you have seen or otherwise observed. No interpretation, no description of how that impacts on their character or shows their cartoonish evil motives. Just the facts.
- Second, describe the conclusions which you have drawn from these observations. This is where you can (politely) describe what you have thought, felt, or attributed based on their actions.
- Lastly, ask them for their perspective, and what they think of your conclusion and observations.

Note that you're not trying to persuade them of your viewpoint or getting them to agree with you, it's about learning their perspective and understanding their thoughts.

Most times this will lead to some sort of awkward discussion, even if you do it correctly. Make sure you remain fully involved in the conversation and avoid closing it down. Many people will respond to a stressful topic by either avoiding it (withholding information, staying silent, changing subjects, leaving the room) or becoming aggressive (shouting, threatening, otherwise attempting to force their viewpoint on people). Either of these will stop any hope of working out your issues, so watch out for the warning signs and avoid them at all costs.

Keep a safe environment for discussion

In general, if you're trying to have an important or tough conversation, you want everyone to be fully involved and willing to compromise. This means they have to feel safe, rather than spending all their time examining your words for hidden insults or threats. Safety doesn't come about by magic, you have to actively put work into making the right environment with your words and actions.

Does this sound kind of wishy-washy? In a way, yes, but it works. And there are several concrete ways you can act which will help build this environment.

- Use 'we' instead of 'I' and 'you'. It's a simple change, but it significantly increases buy-in from everyone involved

Interacting with others

- Go in with an assumption that the opinions and needs of everyone involved will be respected. This helps shape your actions, even subconsciously.
- Use contrasting statements. Explain what you don't intend for the conversation (assigning blame, etc.) then directly afterwards explain what you do want to get out of it (solutions, ways forward)
- Create a sense of mutual purpose, something which all involved can focus on when opinions are differing. This may not be the best solution, but it gets ideas rolling and may at least give you a compromise solution. How does it work:
    - Point out, actively, that the groups are at cross-purposes. State openly that you would like to find a better option for all.
    - Clearly decide what your underlying goal is, being careful not to confuse what you *want* with *how* you want to get it. Your goals (or purpose) are more important than the process that delivers them to you.
    - Get everyone to pile in and try to find either a common goal (no matter how small) or common long-term purpose (i.e. a 'higher' hope that they have).
    - Now brainstorm for different ideas which would push you towards that common goal/purpose.
- Be an active listener, because everyone likes to feel that someone cares about their problems. Ask for their opinions and thoughts, be genuine and show interest in what they say. Paraphrase what they say into your own words to show that you're taking in their information. And then push them to provide more details by taking a guess at their underlying meaning – even if you're wrong, they'll inevitably correct you and include more information.
- If you're listening to what others are saying, then *listen*. Don't try to debate or prove yourself correct.

Define the action you will take

Having a tough conversation, working through problems, and learning each other's opinions are all completely useless if you don't actually do anything afterwards. This is why the end of the conversation is just as important as the beginning and the middle.

At this stage you should nail down what has been decided, how it will be implemented, and who will do it. This should be documented (meeting minutes, etc.) and followed up to ensure that something has actually occurred. A nice overview to keep in mind is "who does what, and by when?"

Following up on the outcome can be difficult if you don't want to appear like a micro-manager. It's generally better to take a softer approach such as setting regular update meetings or defining milestones which need to be met. In general, people will only feel accountable for a task if you give them the opportunity to say that they have done it – use this natural desire to show off to encourage them to do the work.

9. Dealing with managers

A close relationship with your boss is the key to your career success. They are the main driver of any decision on promotion or bonuses, they are the ones who will enthuse about you when 'good' projects are coming up, and they are the ones who will protect you when something goes wrong.

It is thus very important to figure out what your boss needs from you, whether it be skills, connections, or the right personality, and *provide that to them*. Don't be afraid to put on a different persona, don't worry if you aren't representing yourself perfectly accurately. Once you have a solid connection to your boss, then you can start showing more of the real you. Until then, act.

At the same time, it's important to not be obviously better than your boss. Few are able to avoid jealousy when dealing with a more-talented counterpart, and it's even more difficult when that talent is working for you. So be talented, but focus that talent on achieving your bosses' goals and making them look good. Ensure that everyone knows you are doing this, of course, as this will improve the reputation of your boss and you at the same time.

What does your boss need?

Your manager has certain requirements and problems, and solving most of those will require the help of the team. In other words, you and your colleagues. Which means that your 'value' in the organisation is closely linked to how well you solve your *manager's* problems. Note, not your own problems. Theirs.

How do you go about this? There are several things which managers' value, and which you as an employee can provide to improve your situation. Not every manager is looking for the same thing, most will value a few of these in particular. The different possibilities include:

- **Performing beyond requirements**: This is the classic one, but it's still fundamental to building reputation with your manager. Do more than they expect, and they'll value what you can do.
- **Control your area**: If your manager knows that you are in control of your area, then they can focus attention on other problems. Knowing that someone competent is dealing with things is extremely relieving for managers, and they will value you accordingly.

- **Think politically**: A large part of management is dealing with politics within the organisation. A subordinate who also understands this, and who takes politics into account when acting, is both rare and valuable.
- **Act as a sounding board**: A second opinion is always helpful for a manager. Particularly if it's from someone sensible, who will actually think about the idea and provide honest feedback – especially when the idea is terrible.
- **Provide information**: Politics runs on gossip and backdoor channels, and these run through all levels of the company. Keeping your manager up-to-date on gossip and useful rumours running through *your* network is very helpful for both of you.
- **Escalate problems**: Things go wrong, this is expected. But being surprised by a problem, particularly one which has been simmering for a week, is never enjoyable. Being known as someone that will bring the manager in *when necessary*, while solving those problems that you can, is an excellent boost to your reputation.
- **Represent your manager**: Provide an accurate (but positive) representation of your manager in your interactions with others in the organisation. In other words, make sure their reputation spreads.
- **Be creative**: New ideas push processes and businesses beyond their current baseline, they help solve unexpected problems in clever ways, and they make you and your manager look good when they are implemented.
- **Defend decisions to your team**: This is more relevant to those who have a team of their own. You are the translator between your manager and your team –support messages and orders coming down the chain with your own voice. This supports their power, which in turn makes you valued.
- **Take initiative**: Put some extra time into investigating new ideas, jump in to prevent a problem before it occurs. Very, very few people are brave enough to do things on their own – so stand out from the crowd. Your manager will appreciate it.

Keep records

You'll get many requests as you progress through your career, usually asking you to take on additional tasks or head up different projects. Saying yes to the important ones is generally a good idea, and carefully navigating these can see you promoted quite quickly. But rewarding projects are high risk, which means that eventually something will go wrong. And when that does happen, you will find that managers and co-workers will conveniently 'forget' that you asked them to do something, passed on a piece of information, or warned them of the upcoming dangers.

This is why it's important to cover your tracks. Never provide a warning via private conversation, whether it be online or in person. These are temporary and any record will quickly disappear or be lost – and if it wasn't documented, it wasn't done. Any important communication should be via email with multiple people on CC, or in a meeting with multiple attendees. Save a copy of that email in your folders, make sure the information is documented in the meeting minutes. This lets you point to something months or years later, when everything explodes into chaos, and say 'I told you so. Now let me fix your problem'.

Dealing with a new manager

Regardless of where you are in your career, you are going to have a boss. And that boss also has a career, the temptation to find a new position, or even hostile supervisors who may try to force them out. Regardless of the reason, you will eventually find yourself with a new boss. And then you will have to deal with them.

Anyone coming in to a new role will have their own ideas, their own plans to shake-up the current department. They will first spend some time figuring out what to do, who to trust, and how to start. And as part of this initial process they will develop an impression of you, one based on information from the outgoing boss, HR, and your initial discussions. This can either be a good impression, or a bad one. We'll look at both of these in the following sections.

The new boss has a good opinion of you

The new boss might like what you're doing and feel that you're a valuable member of the team. This is great: it's an excellent start and you'll find the change in supervisor comparatively quite simple. But you can't assume things will *remain* this way, your previous successes won't be valued forever and it's expected that you keep improving. The new boss will want new approaches and new wins – anything which distinguishes them from the previous manager. You'll be expected to do more with less, bringing success to the group.

Managing all of this requires careful work on your part – there is a lot to learn about your new boss in a short period of time. Here are a few tips to get you through:

- Figure out what your boss wants from team members – do they like regular updates or ad-hoc meetings when topics arise; quick chats or formal discussion with well-designed slide decks? Once you have figured out what they want, give it to them.
- Keep your boss up-to-date, let them know what you are planning and what you are doing – particularly when it works well. But don't meet *too* often, otherwise you will have less progress to report each time and they will start to think you are coasting.
- Any recommendation or new idea you have should be thoroughly planned out and assessed by you and your team *before* it gets to your boss.
- Don't give advice to the new boss unless they ask for it. This is particularly important when it comes to things which are 'their' responsibility.
- Keep doing whatever you were doing before the new boss came in. It was enough to make you successful before, it will keep you employed now as well.
- Work *with* their new plans, not against them. But do it in a professional way, no-one respects a bootlicker, even if they are helpful.
- Don't make friends with them.

The new boss has a bad opinion of you

Sometimes the new boss comes in with radical plans for the department, and you don't fit in. Your team is no longer cool, you were too close to the previous boss, they don't think you are capable of succeeding in the new paradigm. This puts you in a difficult spot, and you need to decide what to do.

Your first step should be to carefully look at the plans your boss is putting together. Are they really as bad as you think? Are you sure you cannot adapt to fit in? Quitting or moving to a new position is always possible, but you lose a lot of the influence which you have built up in your current role. Unfortunately there is an apparent law of nature that you will only be offered good jobs when you're going well, never when you are about to quit.

Dealing with managers

If you have decided that you can fit into the new approach, then you need to go to your new boss and discuss this. Get their agreement on the idea, make sure that they will provide at least some time to adapt before booting you out. Once you have this, then you should follow the following tips:

- Do the things which you have agreed on, preferably in a way which is beyond expectations.
- Make sure you have a detailed plan for how this will be achieved, ideally in a written or slide-deck format. Make sure your boss sees it and agrees with it before you implement – this stops them immediately firing you as a scapegoat if it fails.
- Be polite and friendly when dealing with the new boss, and make sure you avoid arguments or confrontation.
- Don't criticise the new boss or their plans in meetings, even if they aren't there. The news that you aren't all that loyal will inevitably get back to them, and disloyal team members tend to have short careers.
- It's possible that you may, after some time, realise that you do not support the plans and cannot respect your new boss (you do not have to *like* them, but you do need to *respect* them). This is a sign that you should think about resigning. Life is too short to stay in a miserable role that you hate – just make sure you have a new option lined up beforehand.

Gaining control as a weak player

We cover the many different forms on influence in another section, including the oft-overlooked fact that you have quite a bit of influence over your manager or other higher-ups. But every so often you will enter a situation where you *don't* have much in the way of influence, power, or control. One where you are considered a 'weak player' in the game, one where you would normally be unable to exert any influence.

Thankfully there are ways to gain a measure of control even in otherwise hopeless cases. Here are a few of these approaches:

- **Form coalitions**: One weak player is a victim, many working together are a negotiating partner. Look around the organisation to find others who are similarly affected by this issue and who will have similar interests as you. Find a way to work together to promote your interests – this can be as simple as clearly sitting on one side of a meeting table, as subversive as delaying a project upon which the other players' promotions depend, or as dramatic as a strike.

- **Monopolise important resources**: Some resources, most typically sources of information or knowledge of key issues, are inherently concentrated. For example, it is rare to have more than one true technical expert on a certain topic in the project team, allowing them to strongly influence any decision using their expertise. Similarly, the executive assistant controls access to the manager and thus can block 'unwanted' visitors. These are both cases where a theoretically weaker player controls an important resource, which can be used as political leverage. Try to determine if you have control over such a resource – and if not, figure out how you can.

- **Play emotional games**: Stronger players are people too, and thus (generally) have emotions. By increasing their emotional investment in you and your cause, it is possible to wield more influence than is normally possible. One approach here is to explicitly note your weakness, pushing for sympathetic treatment during your negotiations. Alternatively, use the variety of techniques noted in the Influencing chapter to build rapport and thus deeper emotional ties.

- **Influence third parties**: Although a dispute may be between a stronger and a weaker player, there may be uninvolved parties who can nonetheless influence the process. Identifying those who can influence (or threaten) the stronger player is an important first step, actually building a connection to them is the next. Alternatively you can try bluffing, giving the impression that you have the stereotypical 'friends in high places' – this is risky but surprisingly effective.

- **Sell others out**: Coalitions and connections are only as strong as the weakest link, and the weakest link can often cut a good deal for themselves in exchange for breaking. If you don't particularly care about the fate of the others, or are able to hide your betrayal effectively, then it can be worth holding a private negotiation with the strong player. Just remember that coalitions become stronger the longer they exist – although it is tempting to get the short-term win, you are losing out on the long-term benefits.

Detecting insane managers

One of the unfortunate realities of life is that the higher up the management chain you go, the better your chances of running into someone who is crazy. Not obviously crazy, in the sense of shouting at passing clouds, but crazy in a self-centred, psychotic way. Three personality traits tend to be highly correlated and over-represented in upper management – narcissism, psychopathy, and Machiavellian-like fascination with intrigue. A further trait – obsessive-compulsive micromanagers – tend to predominate in the lower ranks of technical fields, usually seen in experts who have recently been lifted up the ranks.

This is all very well, but you (presumably) aren't a psychiatrist. How do you spot and diagnose these people in the field? That's where the next few sections come in.

Your boss is a psychopath

Psychopaths are those with an inability to empathise with other people, which expands out into a classic list that may remind you of your current manager:

- Superficially charming, with a quick turn of phrase
- Grand dreams and speeches
- A pathological tendency to lie
- No qualms about manipulating others
- A lack of remorse or guilt for their actions
- Superficial emotions
- A general lack of empathy for other people
- Considers failure to be the fault of others

Roughly one percent of the population are psychopaths, which rises significantly in the ranks of upper management. A drive to get your own way regardless of the consequences for others is helpful in moving up the promotion ladder, but many psychopaths find that they are not good enough at hiding their true natures – the promotion stops when everyone realises what they are. Before this happens, however, they make life miserable for those around them – stealing ideas, lying to everyone, destroying the careers of others to boost their own.

To make things more complex, there are also a number of *talented* psychopaths, those who are very good at disguising their true natures and intentions. A high achiever who seems modest and unassuming might just be a good person, they may also be very, very good at hiding their actions. Keep an eye on what they do and what they say to others.

It is difficult to deal with a true psychopath, and you may find it easier to simply find a new position. If you do stay, your first job is to assume that *everything* they say is a lie until it has been independently verified. Your second is to determine what they are saying about you to your colleagues, and then work hard to prove that these are lies. Both steps appear overly paranoid, and indeed they are – but they are often the only way to protect yourself from the constant manipulation and lying.

Your boss is Machiavellian

Machiavelli was the famously pragmatic Italian diplomat, whose advice to princes focused on achieving success via any required means. Machiavellian managers act in the same way and can be found deliberately manipulating others in order to achieve their own aims. They are free of moral systems and emotional commitments, instead focusing on succeeding by whichever means is most effective. Despite this they generally seem reasonable and normal at first glance.

More specifically, they will tend to have the following characteristics:

- They hide their personal beliefs well, readily changing their position or strategy in an argument to whatever is needed
- They are very convincing during discussions, and avoid admitting that they are lying
- They are suspicious of the motives of other people, but do so in an abstract way – they generally will not judge the morality of motives or actions.
- They are happy to exploit others and do not expect reciprocity – a favour given or received stands on its own, with no payback being expected
- They ignore arguments based on rules or the benefits of co-operation if they cannot see a personal benefit
- Most people consider them to be preferable leaders and colleagues

At least some Machiavellian skills are essential for everyone who wants to develop a career – manipulating others is the core of successful office politics and thus your career success. The problem lies with those who are manipulative *and* psychopaths, as they use their persuasive influence to screw over those who they simply don't like. This can lead to exceptionally long and convoluted schemes to achieve their goals, schemes which will often fail due to complexity.

Spotting Machiavellian managers can be difficult, though a good approach is to ask for their read on other people's motives. If they go into a long-winded and convoluted description of what is going on, complete with complex motives and political manoeuvres, then they are probably a manipulator. Or they are accurately describing a very complex political situation – you will need to use some judgement here.

If your boss or colleague does have this sort of focus on intrigue, then you are usually better off trying to stay out of the way. As with psychopaths, assume that everything they say is a lie until you get outside verification. Try to identify their overall goals and appear to be helpful in their attempts to reach them. And don't get too worried – many managers are nowhere near as talented at manipulation as they believe themselves to be.

Your boss is a narcissist
Narcissists believe that they are the greatest thing in the world – the most intelligent, most attractive, most powerful, or most persuasive person around. This inflated sense of self-importance tends to show up in their actions, where they regularly focus conversations on themselves, ignore low-status colleagues, and seek public approval. They are often charming but terrible at developing emotional connections to others.

Everyone has at least a bit of narcissism inside them, and to be honest this is necessary – you need to think highly of yourself to get ahead in the world. The challenge comes when someone is too enthusiastic about their own talent, as this can poison the work environment around them.

Narcissistic charm makes them popular with others and they tend to gravitate towards leadership roles, though they are usually not very good at it due to their risk-taking and compulsive behaviour. This makes a true narcissist dangerous to the organisation, and you will often find yourself dealing with the fallout of their half-arsed decision-making approach. At the same time, their relentless focus on themselves means that they cannot build the professional networks that are needed to advance their interests.

Dealing with a narcissist can be challenging, particularly as they tend to ignore or deflect any information or criticism which they don't want to hear. You can try to hammer the message home via team feedback, many voices are harder to ignore than one. Alternatively you can work with their main desires by promising promotion and praise if they work with you. After all, you already know what they are interested in. Themselves. Try to pitch requests such that the outcome will boost the narcissist's image, preferably publically – and it is even better if you can word it so they sound like an important part of the solution.

In all cases remember that narcissists are usually fragile egos underneath the irritating self-congratulations. Be careful not to push too hard when arguing with them, as you may go one step too far and turn them into an emotional, angry mess. Which is usually funny to see, but doesn't help your long-term goals.

Your boss is obsessive

Managers often like to keep a close eye on events within their department, particularly when new employees are getting settled in. This is normal, and usually moves towards giving the employee more trust and independence as they prove that they can handle it. Obsessive managers, by contrast, attempt to control and manage every single facet of the department – this is the textbook case of micromanagement.

An obsessive manager will often claim that they have high standards, some will use the term 'perfectionist'. Sometimes this is a bonus, particularly in fields where attention to detail and compliance to rules is highly important. However their lack of flexibility and fear of potential failure will stop innovation and development of team members. The constant requirements for status reports and escalation of minor decisions means that they, and you, will spend long days doing very little.

People who act like this are usually not aware that it is a negative – they believe that others are impressed by their level of control and knowledge. Sometimes you can point out the impact this approach has on their social lives, or try to argue the benefits of being 'done' rather than 'perfect'. Sadly this is a very difficult conversation to have, and you may find it easier to work around them rather than with them.

10. Dealing with subordinates

Progression up the corporate ladder will *almost* inevitably bring you into a management position. Although some careers can go far based on personal responsibility alone, the majority will eventually cap out at a reasonable if not amazing level. The subsequent steps will require you to direct multiple efforts towards a single goal. In other words, you will need to *lead*.

Leading is a skill, and like all other skills it can be trained and developed. Those who can lead and manage a team well are a major benefit for any company, and this in turn leads to more importance for you. Which means that if you are interested in developing your career, then you need to work on your ability to lead and manage groups of people.

How do you manage this? The following sections will help you develop this vital skill.

What do you need to succeed?

There are many different organisations and departments and teams. The exact formula to success varies with your circumstances – there is no one-size-fits-all solution to be the best. But some basics are as follows:

- **Success is usually improvement**: In every industry, a successful team is one which does better tomorrow than it did yesterday. This may be sales per quarter, units manufactured per shift, scientific papers published, patients treated – whatever it is, the important thing is that you are improving. Find out what parameter is most important for your team and your organisation, and then focus on improving that.
- **Your team needs to be supported and inspired**: You are a manager, which means that your success will come from your team. Thus you need to provide the support which they require to do their jobs. This can be tangible things – budget, bonuses, office or lab space to work, etc. – but it can also be intangible things which inspire and encourage them to do better – nicer job titles, prestige, public praise.
- **You need to be fair and consistent**: 'Fair' is extremely important for people, and a manager who is seen as unfair or inconsistent in their decisions will be disliked or even hated. Whether it is dividing up budgets or deciding on office space, you need to be clear and consistent in how you deal with your team.

- **Rock the boat, but gently**: You are there to bring in new ideas and new changes, but you have to be careful in how you do it. Too much change or an overly heavy-handed approach can cause your team to turn against you. A well-organised team can get a manager fired with enough work – don't let it happen to you.
- **Keep on top of issues**: Things go wrong, this is expected. Your job is to find out about these problems and then make sure that they are solved. This doesn't mean you solve it yourself, but you need to be sure it is done – if for no other reason that that you will get the blame.
- **Keep on top of unrest**: The team may be unhappy with your decisions or actions, and this can lead to unrest – angry muttering in the hallway, discussion with other managers or HR, attempts to get you fired. You need to know when this is happening, so that you can either find a way to stop it or get rid of the ringleaders.
- **Create pride**: Your team needs to believe in themselves and what they are doing, they need to appreciate the importance of their work and understand that they are doing it as well (or better) than anyone else. Your job is to make them proud of what they can do.

One of your main goals in developing your career is to gain the respect and loyalty of your colleagues and managers. These are not easy to gain, you need to work at it over a long period of time, and a single mistake can lose in a day what took you a year to obtain. In other words, it's a hard goal to achieve. The following sections provide some useful hints to get you on the path.

Developing your leadership personality

Any organisation has its own culture: the way in which people dress, act, come to work, how long they stay, if they do things together or leave right on finish time. This culture develops over time and is incredibly resistant to change. Growing as a leader within the organisation requires you to understand the culture of the department you are in, and modify your own approach to match this.

There are a few general rules which all leaders should follow – they should be competent but not revolutionaries, their style should match the company culture, and they should not allow others to see when they are in trouble. They need to accept that their job is no longer *doing* work, instead they should *delegate* it and supervise their team to make sure it is done.

Dealing with subordinates

Beyond this, the leadership approach you can take will fall into one of three groups:

- The **tyrant** tells others what to do and holds their place by fear. They make many enemies, who will stay quiet as long as things work well, but who will hit them when something inevitably goes wrong. A tyrant needs to be lucky in success and ruthless in removing their enemies.
- The **benevolent dictator** is friendly and liked, but only as long as they succeed. They accept the lonely position at the top and the lack of sympathy when something goes wrong. The benevolent dictator needs to be just as ruthless as the tyrant, but they hide this behind polite facades, think of an 'internal transfers' for unwanted employees rather than outright firing.
- The **committee chairman** appoints others to a committee or organising group, which then goes on to make the actual decisions. They are basically just a figurehead, but can have a long and successful career if they can do it well.

Regardless of which option you end up taking, you need to be consistent in your decisions. Even the nastiest boss is considered acceptable if they are consistently nasty. It is also expected that you will act as a dictator during crisis situations – a leader's job is to lead, particularly when things are going wrong.

Always support decisions from above

There is a dangerous trap which 'popular' leaders tend to fall into, and that is focusing on being liked by their team rather than following requirements from above. This is not to say that you should accept everything from your manager – part of leading a team is that you exert your power to protect them from stupid requirements and foolish work-streams. But when the arguments are over, the bargaining is finished, and the management mandate is in place, then you need to present *and support* the final decision to your team.

Do not try to buy favour by telling the team how stupid the requirement is, do not roll your eyes when discussing it, or openly discuss ways to avoid doing the work. Your lack of support will eventually be noticed by management, and you can expect to lose your position soon afterward.

Making the most of your team

Your overall success is based on the success of your team – you can only take credit for projects which are complete, after all. The earlier sections briefly touched on the basic requirements for being a leader, the following will go into detail on how to inspire and encourage your team.

Basic rules for gaining respect and loyalty

Gaining respect doesn't require you to follow one management style or another, you can be hard-nosed or soft and lovely. It does require you to be consistent, courageous, positive, and dedicated. It also requires you to pull back from some of the perks associated with power, which can be challenging for newly-arrived leaders.

The basic rules to follow are as follows:

- **Treat everyone equally**: Particularly in a management role, you should avoid having favourites within the team, all of them are your responsibility and need to be treated equally (this is naturally very difficult to do, so at least *don't make it obvious* that you have a favourite).
- **Suffer alongside the others**: You shouldn't ask people to suffer hardships which you cannot cope with yourself. If they are working weekends to meet a crash deadline, you should be there as well.
- **Be first in line for hard work and last in line for rewards**: To truly gain respect, you need to show that you are willing to work harder than your team. Inspire by example.
- **Be nice to failures**: People fail at their tasks, there is no avoiding it. Sometimes they will fail at a big, important tasks. It can be tempting to throw them to the wolves, destroying their careers over the failure. Don't. Instead, find them (easier) tasks which they *can* achieve, thereby training them up to the required level.
- **Make hard decisions**: Sometimes you have to make a decision which is hard on other people. This is part of the job. But you should always make them *after* thoroughly considering the consequences.
- **Praise in public, scold in private**: If a team member did well, then tell them in front of the world – let them enjoy the praise and recognition. If they screwed up, then tell them in a private meeting and do it in a neutral, calm way – this prevents them ignoring your feedback due to anger and embarrassment. The exception here is if

you need to punish someone in public as a way to raise team morale (but be careful doing this, it will cause many problems afterwards).
- **Be confident**: Be confident and calm. Even if you have no idea what you are doing, don't let anyone realise it – confidence is just as infectious to others as panic.
- **Control your emotions in public**: The cool, composed leader is far more respected than the one who goes on an emotional rant. If you need to show anger with others, make sure it's controlled anger – and then stop when it is no longer needed.
- **Be consistent**: Employees need to feel fairly treated, and a major part of that is the knowledge that you are treating them consistently. Once you've decided on your management style, stay with that management style. If you provide rewards such as bonuses or better projects, make sure the system for providing them is clear and consistent.

Once you have gained respect, then you will start to gain *loyalty*, the willingness of your team to go through hardships for you. Although respect is built by being a competent leader, loyalty is built by clearly being there for your team – solving their problems and supporting their interests. This will occur even if you follow a harsh, tyrannical way of leading – your team will accept you being a bastard as long as you are *their* bastard.

So how do you build loyalty? Assuming you fulfil the basic requirements (you are competent and successful), you will need to work on the following:

- **Be approachable**: Your team should be able to approach you with their problems. This has a double benefit – not only does your open-door policy earn their loyalty, it lets you discover upcoming issues before they become a catastrophe.
- **Treat people equally**: From the highest manager to the newest worker on your team, you should be willing to treat everyone fairly and equally.
- **Care about your people's problems**: A good manager is a bit like a parent – they listen to the problems, offer advice on how to succeed, smooth over difficulties and encourage people to do their best. And, like a parent, you need to genuinely care about your team. Fake interest is easily spotted, and will remove any goodwill you may have developed.

- **Reward success**: You should be publicly acknowledging and rewarding successes of your team members – and everyone who sees this reward should feel that it is justified. Never provide an outsized reward to a team member simply because you like them more.
- **Be modest**: You are pretty good at your job, but you don't need to go on about it. And when you do screw up, make sure you accept the blame and take responsibility. Don't dump it on your team members.
- **Provide a feeling of order**: Your team want to feel that you are confident and capable. They do not want to hear about your problems or the political fights you are in – they want to know that you are making the important decisions and keeping their jobs alive. Make sure you provide this feeling.
- **Show enthusiasm**: You should avoid showing anger, stress, anxiety and worry. But you can (and should) show enthusiasm for your team members. A little goes a long way – a lot goes even further.

Explain your actions

One of the biggest points to remember is that a team works best when they know *why* they are doing things. Your short term and long term plans should be openly discussed with the team (excluding secret information, naturally), as this will help them know where you are going and why you are going there. Everyone involved should have a general idea of what they are working on, when it needs to be finished, and why it is important. Teams which do not have this information will rapidly lose interest and motivation, which in turn means less chances of success.

Even more helpfully, a team which understands the end goal will be able to adapt to unforeseen situations without your input – they will focus on alternatives which bring them closer to the target rather than choosing randomly. There are few things more depressing than a team of smart people who are too scared to take a decision because the manager is away for a day.

Of course, you cannot tell your team the full truth all the time. This is where your previous openness comes into play. By explaining things fully in the past, you build up trust for those times when you can't explain. People

Dealing with subordinates

follow orders when they believe there is a good underlying reason, even if it is not immediately available.

Understand needs and act fairly

It is important that you understand what your team members need and help to provide it. People will achieve incredible things in the face of tremendous adversity as long as they feel valued. How do you create this feeling? It isn't easy, and you will need to work at it over a long period of time:

- **Understand what they want**: Are they focused on promotion, on a reliable set of tasks, on novelty, on pay? Generally most employees want appreciation, recognition, a comfortable environment, or money. This is not always the case, as we discuss in our list of currencies (pg. 155), which means that you will need to... well, actually *talk* to them. Ask questions, float ideas, find out what makes them tick.
- **Match performance and outcomes**: 'Fair' is important to everyone, and team members are no different. Few things destroy motivation like the feeling that the work they do doesn't matter, that it is neither seen nor accounted for later. Ensure that you recognise hard work, and that wherever possible you equate their hard work with a reasonable reward.
- **Make reasonable goals**: Set goals for your team members, make them a bit hard to achieve, but ensure that they are not *too* hard. Reasonable goals with a reasonable challenge will keep people fired up and interested in the work, which in turn leads to far better performance.

Encourage others

A major part of your job is to act as the team cheerleader, to bring your team onto that level of interest and competence where they can solve any problem and beat any deadline. Is this hard work? Yes. Is it necessary to achieve their full potential? Yes. Does your team achieving their full potential reflect exceptionally well on your leadership skills? Also yes.

- **Encourage independence**: You should be both allowing *and encouraging* your team to show their greatness. This means giving them the reins on a project and letting them show what they can do. Sometimes this turns out terribly, of course, and you should be

ready to step in when everything goes off the rails, but you should not step in *before* this point.
- **Act enthusiastic**: Every job has its terrible days, full of pointless meetings and irritating bureaucracy. Inevitably, you will have a team member come up at this point and tell you about a success they had, or a problem which is occurring, or request advice. Not in the mood to care? Tough. Suck it up and fake the excitement, enthusiasm or happiness which they need to see.
- **Save people**: As mentioned before, people will make mistakes, often mistakes which you see coming before they do. When this happens, be sure to warn them of the upcoming tragedy. Although it can be entertaining to see arrogant team members get crushed by circumstances, this usually reflects badly on you as well. Unless you are deliberately trying to get them fired, of course, in which case let the train wreck happen.
- **Immediate feedback**: If you see that a team member has done something good, (or bad), then provide feedback as soon as you can. Feedback provided several weeks after the fact is rarely remembered, even worse is the feedback which comes half a year later in the annual performance review.
- **Say good morning**: This seems kind of minor in comparison to the other points, but being friendly to your team members is an important part of building up their self-confidence. They are more likely to take a risk in a job where the atmosphere is supportive.

Delegate

Delegation is one of the most important skills to learn when leading. No-one is able to do everything themselves. Attempting to do so leads to micro-management and burnout – and most of your team leaving in frustration as well. You need to be comfortable with passing work and responsibility on to your team members, even if there is the chance (or even the high likelihood) that they won't do it the same way that you would.

This can be difficult, of course, so sometimes it helps to think of the main reasons that it's worth delegating:

- **Productivity**: The number of things which can get done will improve significantly. This applies to your team members (as they will now *do* things rather than waiting for approval) and to you (as

you can pass away tasks where you aren't required, leaving time to focus on important things).
- **Supervision**: You now have more time, which means you can concentrate on your real job, that of managing and leading others. Whether it's finding a new team member, organising rewards for team success, or simply keeping track of things, delegation provides time to get it done right.
- **Developing your team**: Team members with no responsibility will never develop their skillset. Those who want to develop will eventually leave, those who don't... are rarely good team members. Delegation allows you to train them in new skills and provide new experiences, which in turn means that you can delegate more work.
- **Increasing job satisfaction**: One of the main predictors of job satisfaction is a feeling of autonomy, the feeling that you are in charge of something. Delegation is a great way to satisfy this need in your team members, while still keeping a close eye on them.
- **Improved evaluations**: It becomes a lot easier to see which of your team members are talented and which are basically useless when you give them varied assignments, particularly those which require a bit of brainpower and ingenuity.

But I can't delegate

Many, many people are bad at delegation and trusting other people. It usually comes from a fear of losing control, that others won't be able to complete tasks as well as they can. Others may worry about the build-up of expertise within the team, specifically the realisation that they are no longer the main manager who knows everything and keeps everyone in line.

This is, to be honest, not how the world works these days. Almost all businesses are highly complex, beyond the scope of a single person to understand and manage – at least if they want to do a good job. Instead you need to accept that a well-connected team with overlapping goals and responsibilities is the main driving force behind any success. Which of course means delegation. Those needing the feeling of control can be happy that they still control the overall direction of the team, but have to step away from day-to-day micromanagement.

So how do you improve your delegation skills? There are a few things to keep in mind:

- **Be clear**: If you want something to be done, then you need to clearly define what it is. Do not simply throw vague ideas out and assume they will be acted upon – truly exceptional employees may be able to manage, but they probably aren't working for you. Give clear goals, though non-specific instructions on how to achieve them. Let your team member figure that part out themselves.
- **Encourage learning**: Some team members will come back to you for advice or decision-making. This is fine, if it happens sporadically. Those who constantly come back to you should be gently encouraged to make their own decisions – learning how to do this is an important skill for everyone.
- **Allow failures**: Delegation is not without risks, and sometimes the person you delegate to will screw things up completely. This happens sometimes. Take all measures needed to keep track of the delegated project, encouraging and gently guiding your team member, but sometimes they need to have a project blow up in their face. Not only is this good for learning, but delegating tasks which are guaranteed to fail is also a long-honoured way of showing cause to fire unwanted subordinates.
- **Start out small**: Many leaders with a fear of delegation developed it due to a specific incident in the past, where an attempt to delegate went horribly wrong. If you are in this situation, it's important to ease yourself back in – start delegating easy, low-risk projects to your more experienced team members. Once you see this succeeding, try to move on from there.

Don't forget the little guys

It is very tempting to focus all of your political efforts on those further up the chain, your managers and those above them. This is a mistake, as the people below you – those with lower-paid or less-strategic jobs – are critical to achieving your goals. This is *not* just the people on your team, you need to think about those who are well outside your chain of command but who are still able to influence your project. Think of the compliance auditors, the IT guys, the secretary. Each of these seems unimportant in comparison to a major business project, but each has significant power in their respective domain. They can speed up or delay tasks which they are responsible for, and can usually do it in a way which seems natural and not-at-all-vindictive.

In other words, smart managers think about everyone who is involved, and do their best to get all of them on side. If you cannot manage this (there

Dealing with subordinates

may be too many, or some might just be arseholes) then find the key ones and focus your attention there.

Use your office

It's rare to see a manager getting their own private office these days, the switch to open-plan and flex-desk setups has removed the dream of a personal space for leaders. But if you are lucky enough to have an office, then you need to put the effort into making it *your* office – a place which will support your role as a leader.

What does that mean? The typical office will have the following:

- **A desk**: The place where you work, obviously, but also a piece of furniture which makes a clear division between 'behind' and 'in front' of the desk. Sit behind the desk to emphasise your power, particularly in conversations where you need to impose your will on others. Come around from behind the desk to create a more level and open atmosphere.
- **Your chair**: It should be comfortable, obviously. Higher chair backs also create the impression of higher rank and importance, although you should not overdo this to the point of looking like a supervillain. Power is also implied by chair height, the ability to swivel, and armrests – hence why so many visitor chairs are small and basic.
- **Guest chairs**: These sit in front of the desk and are there to hold your visitors. They should match the desk (appearances are important), but be very clearly made for people who are less important than you. They also shouldn't be too comfortable, to encourage visitors to leave as soon as the meeting is over. It also helps to make guests sit with their back to the door – this is a subconscious stressor and a great way to disconcert those you don't particularly like.
- **A table for discussions**: If you've the space, a small table with several chairs is fantastic for informal discussions or problem-solving meetings. This is the best place to bring the discussion if you don't want to focus on hierarchy.

If you are far up enough in the hierarchy that you can choose your own office (and assign offices to others) then you need to be careful. Picking the biggest office or most dramatic view for yourself creates an explicit ranking amongst your team, who will compare their own offices in the minutest detail for signs of favouritism. Save yourself the hassle and take something middle-of-the-road, which removes the competition completely.

Alternatively, if you *do* want to create a sense of hierarchy within the team based on offices, then remember the different factors which can be mixed and matches to create the impression of status. Private offices, larger areas of personal space, more luxurious furnishings, a nice desk, windows, and a location near to the 'action' (i.e. upper management) are all considered a sign of status.

Starting with a new team

Any time you come in to manage a new team, people will be worried. Things have changed, people don't like change, they will worry about the impact on their jobs and their careers. They will look at your previous record, look you up on search engines, and gossip for hours around the coffee machine.

It's important to make a reassuring and simple entrance. Think about the leadership style which you'd like to project, and plan to get this style across from the first day. Remember that this is the style you will be using for your entire time in the position, which means you need to be comfortable with it. Team members appreciate consistency, make sure you don't change styles halfway through the year.

You'll inevitably have to give some sort of speech to the new team. The safest approach is to say something nice about the organisation, and something nice about your predecessor (unless they were fired for incompetence, naturally). Be humble but confident in your previous accomplishments, and stress that you will all have the same success in the future. But don't praise anyone but the previous leader and *never* talk about plans to change the team – this applies even if you intend to fire the lot of them.

The first days and weeks will involve a lot of information-gathering. You'll be looking for answers to a number of basic questions:

- **What does my predecessor think?** It's always worth talking to the last person to hold the position. In most cases there will be some sort of formal handover, but a simple chat will also give you much-needed information on the team members, their strengths, and weaknesses. Keep in mind that it will be biased information,

Dealing with subordinates

particularly about their favourites, but you can still work through it to get an idea of the situation.

- **What do my team members think?** Meet everyone in the team for an informal 1:1 chat wherever possible. It takes a lot of time, but gives you a chance to get their (mostly) honest opinions and remove any fears they might have. You'll need to listen to them while still showing that you are an energetic leader with ideas for the future.
- **What is my goal?** Leaders lead, but first they need to know *where* they are leading. Are you taking the team to new heights, reducing it to save costs, pushing into R&D or taking cover until the storm blows over? You'll need to consider all the parameters in your new situation before making a final decision – this is something which can often take several months. But it's important to have a clear, challenging, and interesting goals. Having a small and easily-achievable goal impresses no-one, and your team will not bother to follow along.
- **Who needs to be replaced?** There are inevitably employees on the team who are either incompetent or strongly aligned to the previous leader. You will get an idea of this in your initial 1:1 meetings with the team members, and it will solidify with time. You will need to plan out harmless-sounding transfers to avoid any anger or disloyalty – both from the people you remove and those that remain.

Once you have determined where the team will go in the future, you have to decide how to get it there. Inevitably this requires several employees being moved on to new roles. There are a few ways you can do this:

- Fire all those who do not make the grade for competence or loyalty at the same time. Similar to a Soviet-style purge, this removes the problem employees while terrifying the remainder. Note that you can cause significant damage to the team dynamics by doing this, and very little work will be done during the lay-off period (and beyond).
- Slowly move unwanted people into new positions which have fancy-sounding titles but no real importance. This is gentler than firing but still gets them out of the way, while those who remain will get the message.

- Find the *least*-popular of your unwanted employees and fire them publicly. This establishes you as the powerful tyrant, but can lead to serious problems if the one you fire is more popular than expected.

Regardless of which option you want to go for, it is *very* important to get HR agreement first. Few things will sink your career like a lawsuit based on illegal layoffs, so make sure your arse is covered.

When people want, or need, to go

At some stage a member of your team will leave. This is a common event, and you will need to get used to it. The main question is whether it is a decision from their side or from the company's side. There are essentially three ways by which people will leave their jobs:

- They are being pushed out by management – either asked to find a job elsewhere or transferred involuntarily to a new position.
- They realise that they are about to be pushed out, and so find another job first.
- They are very good at their jobs and so are recruited for another position.

How you handle these three situations will affect the morale of your team and the overall impression people have of your leadership skills.

They are fired or transferred

The employee in question is simply not capable of doing their job, and so needs to be moved out of the company or into another department. The main question to ask is whether it is worth keeping them in the team at all – can they be rescued, or is it a waste of time? If there is no point offering another chance, then this needs to be communicated.

Generally this happens in a private meeting, where it is politely but clearly stated that they need to find a new position by a certain date. Kind managers keep this ultimatum quiet for a while, which gives the impression that they have left voluntarily.

There are two possible outcomes at this point:

- **They find a new job**: And everything is ok, there is a nice farewell party and everyone says how sad they are to see them leave.

- **They can't find a new job**: This may be due to bad luck, overly-high expectations from the employee, or simply that everyone recognises their incompetence. Sometimes managers will find an internal transfer for the employee – off to some little department where they can't screw anything important up. More often, they will simply be let go on the target date. It's hard, but it is also a part of your role as a leader.

They leave before being fired

People who are good at their jobs will rise through the ranks until they reach the point where they are no longer good enough – essentially, they have risen to the level of their own incompetence. Alternatively, they may have reached a point where they are no longer interested in the work the company does – the role is dull, the workload is too high, they have other commitments or want to refocus time. In any event, this has led them to be less dedicated in their job, and it is noticeable. And this is soon going to lead to them being fired.

At this point, smart employees will look for a new job – they will get out of the position on their own terms before they can be kicked out. This is perfectly ok. Do not try and persuade them to stay on, don't feel guilty about them leaving. You can even actively encourage them to leave.

It's entirely possible to kick-start this process yourself, if you're feeling sneaky. Spread the word through head-hunters you know that the associate is already 'on the market' and open for recruiting efforts (even if they aren't). This leads to a flurry of recruitment efforts, which is usually enough to tempt them away from the current firm. Look sad, but don't do anything to match these offers – and soon the associate will leave by themselves.

You may be asked to write a recommendation or provide one to future employers. Focus on their good points and accomplishments, be vague about major failures. But don't ignore them completely – you cannot sell a loser as a winner to others (particularly friends in business) – nothing kills trust like being known as the manager who gives false recommendations.

They get a better offer

This is a more difficult situation, as it usually involves competent team members whose loss will leave a significant hole in your group. It's worth asking if your department is able to match the advantages of their new role – the income, prestige, responsibilities, or career opportunities. If yes, then you need to know *why want to leave at all*. Is it a problem with you and your leadership? Were you overly critical? Did you create an unhealthy environment? Were you too cheap with salary and recognition?

Ask the employee leaving what it would take to keep them. If it is something which you can fix, then try to meet their demands and keep them in your team. If they want something which would cause problems with the other team members, then try to find an acceptable compromise (unless they are much better than their peers, in which case do anything necessary to keep them).

If you cannot match their new role, and it is a step up in their career, then let them go with your encouragement and blessing. And make sure they remain a friend in the future, as they should be part of your ever-growing professional network. Being known as someone who develops exceptional leaders for the company or industry is also not terrible for your career.

11. Building and using a network

There are few things which impact your career like the creation and use of a network. What is a network? Simply a loose collection of people who know you, are familiar with your talents, and like you enough to provide a favour every now and again. Networks can be big or small, wide or deep, but all of them are built one contact at a time.

Countless studies have shown that those who spend more time networking and interacting with others will be promoted faster and enjoy better careers than those who don't. This is partly due to increased knowledge (you hear about new opportunities sooner) and partly due to increased prominence (people will recognise your name when it comes up). Even without the career aspects, a strong network allows you to tap into different skills and perspectives when solving problems or achieving goals. In other words, a network makes you better at your job.

Of course, yours is not the only network in the company – everyone has their own set of informal connections and relationships stretching throughout their colleagues. Sometimes this intersects your network, sometimes it doesn't. Most of the time you won't even be aware of who is connected to who until you say something stupid to the wrong person. It is always a good idea to spend time talking to colleagues and teasing out the connections, watching who goes to lunch with who and who regularly catches up for a coffee or two. This can be painful but will give you a vague idea of the networks which are out there. Enough, at least, to stop you saying something stupid.

Creating networks

You cannot do anything with a network until you have built that network, so your first goal is to get the social connections in place. There are a few basic tips which you should keep in mind here, all of which are explained in more detail in the following sections.

- Networks are built from reciprocal relationships
- You need to humanise yourself
- Don't be afraid to invest time and money into relationships
- Your network should be composed of talented people
- Your network should be flexible
- You shouldn't be afraid to gossip, but not too much

Networks are based on reciprocal relationships

The glue of a social network is the regard that members hold each other in. If people hate you, then no network. If people think you are only taking and never giving, then no network. If people think that helping you is a waste of time, because you will never be able to help them in return, then no network.

This seems simple enough, yet it is amazing how often you will come across the dreaded aggressive networker. You know who they are. The one who cruises around meetings, looking for people who can help their career, always ready to describe the wonders of their current role and say things like "hey, you're in marketing, we could team up on [my project #23]". It's really annoying, everyone realises what they are up to, and pretty soon no-one will invite them to any more parties.

Thus if you want to create a network, you need to think about the *other person first*. Your initial thought when meeting others should be to discover *their* goals and offer to help them achieve it. This focus on the *needs of others* is extremely powerful when building connections. Not only do you make them feel that their needs are important (which builds trust), you begin to tip the balance of favours in your direction. We are all strongly driven by the ideal of reciprocity and want to repay favours which we feel are owed. By helping others first, you tap into this drive and are far more likely to receive the help you need at a later date.

Humanise yourself

As mentioned above, you can only build a network if you are willing to be a normal, social human being. Robotic attempts to mesh with people using tips you picked up from the internet are rarely successful. Instead you need to show a genuine interest in them *as a person*, not just a source of potential gain. At the same time, you need to make it clear that you are coming into the conversation as an open partner, not a manipulator.

Although it seems counterintuitive, one of the simplest ways to do this is to use your *own* name. Introduce yourself, say hi. Use their name once or twice so you remember it, then let it go. Many people have taken the old advice into their hearts ("use their name as often as possible, people like hearing their name!") and then overused it – which means that networking events fill with repeating names ("John, I was thinking… that's right John… no John, you mean"). Again, we have an instinctive aversion to this kind of

Building and using a network 147

speech, it seems fake and obviously designed to sell us something. So stand out from the pack, don't overuse their name, and feel free to use yours.

Don't be afraid to spend time or money
You shouldn't be afraid to spend money on building your network. Invite people for coffee or dinner, give a little gift every so often when you catch up. The feeling that you can 'just do' something like this makes you seem more impressive – only a successful guy would be able to casually drop some money on a meeting, right? Not necessarily, but how it *looks* is the important thing. Not only do you gain an aura of success, but you create a feeling of obligation in others which they will then subconsciously need to repay.

Money is not the only currency out there, with time being arguably even more valuable. Providing others with access to your time, particularly when it is free of distractions, is a powerful gesture – and this is even more significant when they know how exceptionally busy you are. Take time out to help others, to introduce them to meaningful contacts, to help solve their problems. Just make sure that your time is never undervalued – people who do this will rarely reciprocate.

Focus on talent
Of course, a network is only as useful as the people in it, and if you surround yourself with a network of morons and losers then your career is going to take a dive as well. Look for talented people, either at work or in your personal life, and keep them in your life. Hang out, talk about problems, offer solutions or help – whatever you do, make sure that you are surrounded by talent. Because only a talented network will help you reach your goals.

This is not to say that you refuse to talk to anyone less than a VP. In fact, people with supposedly unimpressive titles such as 'secretary' or 'administrative assistant' are amazingly important. They are direct gatekeepers to your potential career boosters, they understand how things are *really* done in the company, and they can solve any number of bureaucratic problems if they like you enough. Always, always be friendly to the secretary.

A nice way to quickly identify how important someone is in a discussion or negotiation is to look at the pronoun they use. People who are higher up tend to identify more with the company (and seek to downplay their importance during a negotiation) – they will use terms like "we" and "us" more often. People who aren't so important inevitably use "I" or "me" in conversation as a way to make themselves feel better.

Develop flexible networks

Regardless of who you are, a strong network is invaluable to your career. But many people fail to understand what a 'strong' network is – they assume that by forging contacts with many people, it will automatically create a winning set of connections. This is, sadly, not quite right.

A network requires breadth and variety to fully achieve its purpose. This is difficult. Most people will automatically end up with a network of people just like them – they work in similar jobs, probably met at the same organisation, have similar hobbies. This is natural, we create connections at work and we like to keep in touch with those who have similar interests. But this creates a dense and highly interconnected network, one which will tend to share viewpoints and information sources. In other words, they become an isolated echo chamber, in which everyone is equally vulnerable to incoming layoffs or changes to the field.

Although a dense network is helpful in your day-to-day work, it cannot provide the information and opportunities that a broad network would offer. Thus it is critical to spread your connections out – to other levels of the career ladder, to other departments in the company, to other companies in the same and different fields. The wider your reach, the better off you will be.

Your time to network is limited, naturally, so you should think of it in terms of weak and strong connections. Spend the majority of your time forging strong bonds with a small core group – usually those who are fairly related to your current position and can help you with your current needs. But set aside time to develop weak bonds with those other, broader connections. It doesn't need to be much, a coffee every quarter year or so, but enough to keep the contact going and to pass on any useful information which you might have.

Another aspect of this which many people forget is that you need to retain good relations with those you have passed by as well. Careers are long and tricky things, and the person you stabbed in the back to get this promotion may end up as your manager at a later date – or even worse, have well-placed connections in the company. Keep friendly connections with everyone as you move along, even if they are 'below you'.

Gossip

Every company has gossip. There have been many attempts to promote an open organisation with free information flow, but it very rarely works to stamp out the underground grapevine. And why? Because gossip works. Gossip is a way to gain information via informal channels, skipping the 'expectation management' which so often colours official announcements. It provides non-official information on co-workers – their strengths, weaknesses, interests, etc. It allows us to express our anger (or happiness) at ongoing events. And it is an indirect way to bring up or continue conflict with others.

Gossip is an effective approach in highly-political organisations, providing you with back-channel influence and information which is otherwise hard to obtain. The challenge is that gossip takes away the desire to improve the situation – it's easier to complain to others than to solve a problem, and assuming that you can *only* use unofficial channels of influence scares you away from trying to use an official one.

This means that you should be careful about the use of gossip. By all means insert yourself into the network, find trusted colleagues and use it as a way to gather all the information you can. But treat all information as biased (because it is) and avoid the temptation to vent about things you don't like. That's just a weakness.

Keep track of your network

Once you have a network (or at least the beginnings of one) then you need to start keeping track of it. Socially organised people tend to do this by instinct, chatting with a wide range of contacts continuously and subconsciously knowing when they haven't heard from someone for a while. The rest of us need to be slightly more organised in how we run things.

One extremely effective way, if a bit of overkill for the normal network, involves a formal tracking and catch-up system, as explained below:

- **Set up a tracker**: Your first step is to set up some sort of system for tracking everyone in your network. Some people use the contact list in their phones, others use paper-based lists, yet others have a large spreadsheet. The important thing is that you have somewhere to write down: who your contact is, where they work, in what role,

when you last contacted them, and any additional notes you may have on them.
- **Fill the tracker**: Put the details of all your professional contacts into the spreadsheet. Fill in any interests or common hobbies which you might have into the notes section. Your aim is to have a central location where you can quickly look up people and remind yourself what your next discussion should cover.
- **Determine contact periods**: How often do you want to keep in contact with each member of your network? A nice rule of thumb is that you should drop a line to the important ones at least a month, the middling ones at least once a quarter, and the comparatively irrelevant once a year.
- **Schedule times to contact them**: Yes, this sounds a bit silly, but you should be scheduling your network-contacting duties. If you don't then it rapidly becomes a low-priority task, then a task that you will get to when you have time, then one you should have done last week, then a faint memory of something that you should have done. Want it done? Set reminders.
- **Keep it updated**: A tracker is only as useful as the accuracy of the information. Take care to keep the tracker updated as your contacts change companies, careers, phones and addresses – otherwise you will find that it steadily diminishes in value as the years go on.

Nurture your network

So you've created a network, and now it's time to develop it – to become more than just 'that guy I met once' and instead be seen as an interesting and anticipated contact. How do we do this? Using the simple method which we mentioned before, the power of helping others and developing reciprocal relationships. It's important to occasionally provide things to your contacts which they will find valuable. Note that *they* need to find it valuable – if it's interesting to you but irrelevant to them, it's a waste of time.

What sort of things can you provide?

- **Useful information**: There is a vast amount of information out there and no-one can keep track of it all – hence the appreciation when receiving a useful bit of information from others. The stereotypical example here is a link to an article which you have read, always with a short summary attached to help them place it in context. You can either do this spontaneously (forward the article as soon as you read it) or in batches (keeping track of many interesting articles, then forwarding on to several people who may be interested at once). The more dedicated approach to this is to provide notes of books which you have read and which you think may be relevant to them. Be careful with this one, however, as a long, sprawling, and badly-written summary can do terrible things to the impression of competence you are trying to build.

- **Congratulations**: Everyone likes to hear when they have done something well, so why not pass it on to your network? Whether it is a new job, a major project completion, even a well-received and difficult presentation, take the chance to say congratulations. This keeps you in their mind, reinforces the connection, but deliberately doesn't make any request for help – the ideal way to nurture your network. Just make sure you are *specific* in saying what you liked rather than sending a bland 'well done'.
- **Thanks**: You should take the chance to say thank-you whenever they have helped you. Interestingly, this doesn't necessarily require *direct* help, you can always thank them for providing inspiration through one of their actions, which in turn motivated you to achieve one of your goals.
- **Get-togethers**: As your network grows, it will become more and more difficult to catch up with everyone on a 1:1 basis. A simple way to work around this is to set up small gatherings for contacts who know each other – members of your previous office, for example. This means that everyone knows each other, has something to talk about, and will remember you as the one that brought them all together.
- **Connections**: Everyone knows someone, and that connection may be valuable to yet another. Talk to your contacts, ask about their problems and find out what sort of connections they are looking to make. Then find the appropriate person within your network and put the two in touch. Keep in mind: every time you do this you will gain (or lose) reputation based on the outcome – only introduce contacts if you believe there is a real chance that they will find value in each other.

Entertaining others

As part of your career, you will inevitably end up entertaining other members of the company. These may be your superiors, your equals, various important guests, or your team members. Naturally there are different 'rules' to follow depending on who and how you are entertaining, but the most important one is constant: be consistent with yourself – your own sense of style, personality, and interest.

The following sections go over this in more detail.

Entertaining superiors in a restaurant

The first step is to determine what their taste involves – do they like sushi, Italian, a plate of BBQ ribs? If their taste is very different to yours, then find a compromise which will work for both. There's no point going to a restaurant you despise in an attempt to impress upper management – your discomfort will be obvious and will distract you from your 'duties'.

The ideal choice of restaurant is one which is fairly upper-class, neither ridiculously expensive nor cheap, matches their interests or tastes, and reflects the personality you are trying to project (competent and secure in your style). If you have a matching restaurant where you are *known*, where you can be greeted by name and taken directly to your table, then you are even better off.

Try to follow a few simple rules of thumb:

- A private room is only needed if you are discussing confidential business matters, for any other situation it looks weirdly overdone.
- Drink in moderation, preferably wine (it looks better). If your superior doesn't drink, then do the same. If you are having lunch, then don't drink – the days of boozing with the boss are long past.
- There is no such thing as a purely social event – your ability to entertain *will* be linked to your ability to work. Make sure you are able to keep conversation flowing, preferably on a topic which they find interesting (this may require research beforehand).
- Don't tell them any bad news – it's guaranteed to ruin the evening. If you are having a business lunch, then keep the serious topics until the end of the meal.
- Dress up – you want them to think that you are a professional. No shorts or tracksuit pants.
- Plan the seating order carefully. Guests will want to sit next to you (the host) or your superior (the VIP). Make sure you do not group 'important' people at one end and leave the less-important at the

Building and using a network

other – they will notice, and they will be irritated. Instead, try to mix senior and junior guests to force a bit of variety.
- In general only 4 people can participate in a conversation at a table, so plan the social groups around this.
- Don't give a speech or a lecture to the group. If you absolutely have to, never praise the restaurant or the food – if it weren't amazing, you wouldn't have chosen it.

Entertaining superiors in your home

This is a more complicated scenario than a restaurant, you will need to appear spontaneous and natural while still planning everything in detail. The general tips in the previous section apply here as well, in addition you should also consider the following:

- Assuming the main guests are you and your superior (plus partners), you should aim to have 1-2 other couples along for an entertaining evening.
- When choosing the other guests, try to ensure there will be shared interests and no major clashes in political or religious beliefs. They should also be able to entertain and keep the conversation flowing.
- You can consider getting a catering company to do the cooking and serving. It isn't ideal, as it takes away the 'home-made' feeling, but leaves you free to chat rather than serve food.
- Plan the meal based on the likes and dislikes of your guests. Make sure the food and drinks are high quality and (most importantly) taste good.

Entertaining equals

The general approach to entertaining others is perfectly applicable to anything you do with your equals. The main difference is that you'll never discuss business matters (this is what daytime meetings are for), your aim is to strengthen the bonds between the guests. Obviously you aren't trying to weasel your way into some sort of networking event, but simply creating a relaxed and sociable atmosphere will improve your relationship with others. Which leads to a stronger personal network. How convenient.

Entertaining subordinates

This is one of the more difficult events to pull off well. Regardless of what *you* think, the others will always think of you as their boss. So don't pretend to be friends or best buddies, this is doomed to failure, instead work on making everyone feel at ease and comfortable to be around you.

Seem complicated? It is! Here are a few tips to help get through:

- You'll generally be entertaining a group of people at once. You need to decide up front if partners are invited or not – as a rule of thumb a family-oriented company will involve partners, one which just wants to celebrate with colleagues will not.
- Be friendly and pleasant, feel free to make a few jokes. But never make jokes at their expense, because they cannot respond equally (you are still their boss tomorrow, after all).
- If you're going to a restaurant, choose one which is nice and comfortable for your team – don't pick the fanciest place around in an attempt to impress them.
- You should be able to remember everyone's name. If you are head of a very large department where it's not feasible, then you can have nametags for everyone. This is easier to do if several departments are celebrating together, or if non-work-related partners are invited. Otherwise it's fairly obvious that you don't know who everyone is.

12. Influencing others

Some power is derived from your position or your authority – you have people who work for you, and you can 'simply' tell them what to do. But the corporate world is changing, and many of us are now in flat or 'matrix' organisations, ones in which you need to influence people who are entirely separate from your department and hierarchy. This requires a different, more calculated approach to influencing, one which you will likely need to practice. This chapter covers the do's and don'ts of this process.

Always plan first

You should begin by thinking of your eventual goal – what are you intending to achieve with any use of influence? Generally there are a number of targets to be influenced in order to reach our goals, which means that it is important to take a moment to work out a game plan.

Evaluate your connections

Think carefully about each person who you are in contact with and identify those who can help with an upcoming goal. What are the main factors to consider here?

- How well do you know them?
- What is your current opinion of them?
- How can you approach them, if needed?
- How does your personality, background, and working style mesh with theirs?
- Do you have opposing personalities? If so, how could you improve your relationship?
- How could you adapt your work style to collaborate with them?

Decide on your goals and priorities

You need to decide what your needs are before trying to persuade anyone of anything – after all, you can't communicate what you want, if you don't know what it is.

Sit down, take a pen and paper, and make a list of your primary goals. Then prioritise them – which are most important to you? Which are less important but will allow other goals to be realised? Which are nice to have and which are essentials?

These primary goals should be further cut down based on the person you are trying to influence – it is pointless trying to persuade them to your side when they cannot help you in any material way. The following questions may help clarify your priorities:

- What is the time-frame of each goal, short or long-term?
- Do I expect that this person will be able to help in the time-frame of these goals?
- Are the goals essentials, or just things which would be nice to have?
- Given the previous, is it more important to achieve this goal or to retain a good relationship with the person I'll be influencing?

Be sure to separate what you *desire* from what you *need*. This is important to avoid losing your task-related goals amongst the chaos, and prevents you being influenced by the desires of others. Remember that you aren't ignoring all of your wants, just being clear on priorities.

It's also important to remember that your primary goals can be achieved in many different ways, and that a bit of flexibility in planning and adapting may get you there faster than otherwise possible. Follow the essence of your goal, but look at alternatives as the discussion and negotiation goes on.

Choose who you will target

Once you have an overview of your network and your overall goals, then it is time to decide *who* you will be influencing. Of course you can simply try to influence everyone that is vaguely involved, but spreading your efforts like that will be time-consuming and ineffective. Instead, choose two to three people who you believe are truly capable of helping you reach a goal – base this on their power within the organisation and alignment with your needs. Then work out how to persuade them.

How strong is your relationship?

The relationship you have with your person-of-interest is very important for the eventual approach you take to influencing them. A good relationship makes everything easier, you can trade off the existing good-will to enter a clear and straightforward discussion. Mediocre relationships may require some light discussion or preliminary persuasion before you move into the main point. If the relationship is bad, you'll want to spend some effort improving it before you try anything clever.

Influencing others

The quality of any interpersonal relationship is based on a number of factors, but the most important ones in the office are your working style, personality, and background.

- **Working style**: Look around any office and you'll see clear differences in working style. Some prefer freeform creativity and a lack of structure, others want detailed analysis and well-defined approaches. You need to tailor your approach to their favoured working style. And you need to know your own style, because otherwise you'll forget to consider the approaches which are 'foreign' to you.
- **Personality and background**: Your background forms an important part of your personality, built as it is on your history, values, preferences, and goals. Naturally, this is also the case for anyone you are trying to influence. Think about your personalities, whether they mesh together, and whether you can do something to improve the relationship.

What do they need?

This requires you to think about the needs and requirements of your counterpart, and you may also want to observe their behaviour and ask a few questions to ensure that you understand correctly.

What are the main factors which you should be determining?

- **What are their work tasks and responsibilities?** This will directly affect the rewards which you can offer. In addition, it helps to know of any upcoming deadlines – this will reduce the support they can give you, but will also make any help you provide seem much more valuable.
- **Who do they interact with in the firm?** Everyone they interact with will have their own set of requests and priorities, and you may find yourself bumped from the list because the CEO just demanded something.
- **How is their performance measured?** We all have targets, and we're all willing to help others if that helps meet our targets. Which means the value you offer should play into this need.
- **How do these measurements translate into rewards?** Higher pay, share options, longer holidays, etc. Knowing this lets you tailor

an offer – it may not directly help their performance, but perhaps you can provide one of the subsequent rewards instead.
- **What are their career goals?** Much like performance, offering something which can enhance a colleagues' career is a very powerful temptation.

This is all great, of course, but how exactly should you find this out? Essentially, it is a mix of researching them, asking questions, and observing their behaviour.

Observation is an important skill for you to develop during your career, particularly when it comes to those you need to influence or negotiate with. Look beyond the words which they use and look at the subconscious clues which we all display. This includes such areas as:

- **Body language**: Body language provides more information than words do. The mixture of physical gestures, posture, and expression will provide a glimpse into your counterpart's mood – which in turn lets you head off any negative feelings they may have.
- **Word choice**: The language we use is heavily biased by our backgrounds and our interests – managers with a clear focus on cost-cutting will talk about KPIs and budget, sport-loving managers will use phrases specific to their game. These word choices give you a hint of their personal or business background, allowing you to tailor your approach.
- **Tone**: How we say things is often more important than what we say. A lack of interest or inspiration will generally be obvious in the tone of voice, a willingness to hear your offer as well. Sensitive topics will be discussed in a quiet tone, one which should be praised in a louder one. Keep an eye out for this to determine your best approach.
- **The concern which is raised**: If your counterpart raises a concern, this is (usually) an important topic for them. Seems obvious, right? Yet many of us forget this while focusing on how to 'influence' our counterpart – ignoring the fact that the easy answer is right in front of us. Ask them about their concern, show that you care about it and try to find out where it is coming from. You may be able to find an unknown need of theirs within a single exchange.

What 'currency' is in play?

In any negotiation or attempt to influence, there are a number of different factors in play. A very important factor involves the 'currencies' which are being traded back and forth between the different parties. 'Currency' is more than just 'cash' (although it can also include cash) – a currency is anything which is *valued by someone and which can be traded*. In any group of people there are a multitude of different currencies which may be in play, and knowing which of these you can offer or trade is extremely important for planning your influencing.

As a general rule you can divide currencies into five different categories which cover different requirements: inspirations, tasks, position, relationships, and personal. Different people place different levels of importance on these categories, so it's important to assess which ones are most valuable to you and your counterpart.

Inspiration

Inspiration currencies draw on our need to move beyond basic needs and wants, doing things because they fulfil us. These may include:

- **Vision**: Being part of a task which is significant, one which is beyond the daily routine and is important for the organisation, department, or even society as a whole. This is a good way to motivate people beyond their normal efforts, but you need to find the right goal – anything too small will fail to inspire.
- **Excellence**: Being able to do something important (or even not that important), really, really well. The fast-paced world of the office often prevents people from creating the high-quality work they desire, so an explicit chance to do so is often jumped on.
- **Moral correctness**: Doing something because it is *right*, not because it is expedient. This is a higher requirement than the usual 'efficiency at work', and allows those who achieve it to feel better about their lives as a whole.

Tasks

These are the currencies which allow us to do our jobs better, regardless of what those jobs involve on a practical level. These run a wide range, and may include the following:

- **New resources**: Whether it be personal salary, an improved budget, more people in your team, or a larger office, this the

currency which directly improves our position. Particularly in resource-strapped organisations (i.e. most of them) this is a valuable proposition.
- **Challenges**: Having the chance to do hard tasks, which push them to their limit and thus improve their overall skills. This is sought after by highly-motivated or otherwise driven workers, and is a very practical currency to offer – in general it isn't hard to find a challenge to dump on someone else.
- **Assistance**: Not the same as a permanent addition to your team, this is the ability to have assistance for difficult project or even the ability to delegate annoying and unwanted tasks to someone else. Think of this as the lower-key version of providing additional resources.
- **Organisational support**: Support from others in the company, whether obvious or subtle, which helps you push your goals through to completion. People who are highly influential or act as favour-brokers base most of their power on this.
- **Speed**: The ability to get something done quickly is often a rare and valuable currency in a large organisation. Feel free to point out how you are speeding up their solution, but don't overdo it.
- **Information**: Information and knowledge are power, whether it be technical knowledge or just a new source of rumours. Given that most offices run on a mixture of gossip and coffee, having an unusual or inside source of information can be a powerful trading position.

Position

While task-related currencies are focused on your ability to do your job, a position-related one changes how you fit into your role as a whole. This covers such areas as:

- **Recognition**: You do good work, and you'd like to be recognised for it. This is true for everyone, and that's why recognition for success or abilities is such as powerful reward. Which is why it's quite surprising that many managers try to hog the limelight rather than spreading it out to team members.
- **Visibility**: The chance to have your work seen by those in upper management, with the corresponding possibility to move upwards

in your career. This is most useful for those with long-term career plans, but you have to ensure that only the best side of you is visible.
- **Reputation**: Improving your reputation, so that you are seen as committed, competent, or even just clever. Reputation has an overarching effect on almost everything in your workplace life, so being able to improve this is a valuable bargaining chip.
- **Importance**: Being known as someone who is important, whether this is a simple restatement of your current importance or the act of *becoming* important. It is rather ego-driven, but nonetheless widespread.
- **Contacts**: Networks change your ability to do everything, and thus the chance to make new contacts can be very powerful. It is best suited for those who appreciate and control a large network, as they are most likely to be excited by the possibility.

Relationship

These currencies relate to other people, in particular how you deal with them and how they deal with you. It may include such options as:

- **Understanding**: The act of having someone listen to your problems and understand why they are important to you. Interestingly this doesn't necessarily involve providing advice – sometimes people just want to complain.
- **Belonging**: We all like to feel part of a group, of something bigger than ourselves. Being able to offer this is a big draw for some, though it is of course irrelevant for those who prefer to work alone.
- **Personal support**: Having back-up from others for your personal or emotional problems; even if they seem insurmountable. As with understanding, you don't need to solve their problems, but you do need to help.

Personal

These are currencies which apply directly to you, or to whoever you are speaking to. They do not focus on relationships or jobs or anything like that, it's just you. They include:

- **Gratitude**: Receiving thanks for help or services rendered. It seems simple, but is often forgotten in the daily workplace – and worse, the more often you throw it out, the less value it retains.

- **Ownership**: Knowing that you are the owner of a task or project feeds into our deep-seated desire to lead and control events in our lives. This is a useful currency for employees when you cannot pay them more, but do have leeway to increase their personal responsibility.
- **Self-actualisation**: Having your values and identity confirmed or praised is important for our feeling of self-esteem and self-worth.
- **Comfort**: Challenge is all very well, but sometimes we just want to enjoy some comfort – avoiding problems, hassles, and nuisances. Those who strongly value comfort tend not to be high-flyers, but they are often good at their particular niche and will reward you for keeping them safe.

Trading back and forth

One of the challenges of influencing is that there are many, many different things which you *could* offer, but only a small subset which your counterpart will be interested in. This gets even more complicated when you need to determine the *value* of your offering. Is a helpful word in the bosses' ear worth getting information on the new contract? How many favours on IT support do you get for wrangling the group an additional FTE? Given there is no easy conversion to cash, everything becomes a matter of personal belief and interest.

So how do you know what to trade? The first rule – *their* values are more important than *your* values. You may be in possession of the world's greatest model train paint collection, but this is useless if they have no interest in trains, modelling, or paint. You need to determine what is important to your counterpart *before* you look into what you can offer.

Some things are fairly universal desires (to have influence, to receive praise or credit, fair treatment, and a good reputation) yet even here the relative weighting of each can vary significantly from person to person. You will need to analyse their interests and needs to identify the right currency to offer. Look at their job requirements, their current problems, and the things they talk about or seem to value. What are their KPIs, and how are they rewarded for exceeding these? Most of the time you will need to make inferences and guesses, though some people will tell you outright if you ask directly.

Influencing others

This is made harder by organisational politics. Companies generally frown on employees who bargain purely for their own interests, instead requiring any request to be placed in terms of 'benefit to the company'. Watch out for overly-polite or reserved companies – although the political fighting is just as nasty, all of the *requests* will be hidden behind several layers of camouflage. Learning to decipher these is vital for understanding what others need.

One way of estimating this is by looking at the position which the other person holds, and evaluating it based on several factors:

- **Main interaction**: Are they predominantly dealing with people or things? People managers have specialised requirements and the hassle of maintaining FTEs and budgets. Those who deal with 'things' are more likely to be technical experts or specialists in an area.
- **Variety**: Are they doing varied work, or is it the same thing day after day? Repetitive work tends to argue for a comfort-driven mindset and associated values, those doing varied work need a wider range of connections and assistance.
- **Originality**: Do they need to improvise original solutions, or aim for reliable, reproducible accuracy? Original solutions are usually stop-gap measures for emergencies, and so these people tend to prioritise speed or assistance over longer-term currencies.
- **Power**: Do they tell others what to do, or are they told what to do? Powerful roles always appreciate more resources, those without power are often looking for an initial step onto the management/leadership ladder.
- **Risk**: Are they in a risky but visible role, or a comfortable but low-key one? This is tightly tied to ambition, as those in visible roles tend to be aiming for ever-more-visible ones. You can also estimate their ambition from the previous roles they have held – fast track movers tend to stay for a short period of time in successively improving positions. This also means you have a limited time to impress or trade with them, they will be off to a new role within the next year.
- **Dependence**: Do they control everything they need to get things done, or are they a matrix manager reliant on others? Information and assistance are far more useful to the second than the first.

- **Uncertainty**: Do they deal with uncertainty every day, or are things predictable? A certain degree of uncertainty is inevitable, but some jobs run on the edge of chaos every day. Being able to offer a sense of control over even a small part of their role can bring them over to your side.

You can temper these initial assessments using your knowledge of their personality and the organisation as a whole. A rapidly growing company has different worries to one which has been stagnating for decades, and it is even more different in a company which has hit economic problems and will likely be downsizing soon. Organisational culture plays a role, as does the ambition and drive of the person you are looking into. Does their history suggest that they are competent, a political player, a tyrant brought in to upturn everything? All of these will come together to help you estimate their valued trade items.

Trading strategies

Trading favours is difficult because there is no clear medium of exchange, everything comes down to the value which people assign in their heads. To make things even more complicated, it is rare that you will see a single, one-off trade in favours. Instead most trades happen as a series of gives and takes over a long period of time. Which means that you always need to keep an eye on what you *currently want*, and how you will *maintain the relationship* going forward. Think long-term, not just of the here-and-now.

There are a few basic strategies which you can follow when trading favours.

If you get along well and each have something which the other wants, then you have a **simple swap**. This is the easiest of all options, and can use basically any tradeable favour as long as they are considered equivalent by the parties involved. There are no implied long-term debts, you are both free to come back and swap again another time. Make sure you understand *why* the currencies should be considered equivalent, as you may need to persuade your counterpart of this fact.

If your interests match but you lack a tradeable currency, then you must show them that co-operation helps **achieve their goals**. Look at your counterpart and your request, and find a way to reframe that request in a way which is clearly a desirable benefit for them. Make sure you tailor the request to their main priorities for maximum chances of success.

Influencing others

If you are clever enough to find some (believable) unexpected benefits, then you have to sell the idea of **added value**. This is value which comes beyond the normal savings in FTE's and expenses, and includes more abstract fields such as turnover, employee retention, customer loyalty or process improvement. As most of these are abstract it is relatively easy to find *something* that will support your proposal, though successfully persuading others that it is worthwhile may be more difficult.

And lastly, if you have nothing they want, then you need to **compensate them** with 'some other' currency which may be acceptable. Here you accept that they will have to do something for you, but cannot clearly show a benefit to them. Instead you essentially pay them off by offering something else in return, usually over a longer period of time.

You have more influence than you think

It is pretty common to hear the complaint of the lower-level employee – no-one listens to them, they have no power, the political plans of the great move like ocean waves, tossing them to and fro. This is not always the case, and you usually have far more influence than you realise.

Remember that even the most banal job still hides a number of different sources of influence. You may be an expert within a field – this may be relevant for your job (great) or relevant for another job (time to look for cross-over opportunities). You may have knowledge of the organisation – who does what, who is making a play for a certain role, who is doing something interesting, who is sleeping with who? Office politics runs on gossip as much as it does planned persuasion, and everyone can get involved in information sharing. You may be in direct contact with customers and thus hear their problems and preferences first-hand. Most people in upper management haven't seen a customer for years, so this view from the ground can be surprisingly valuable if you sell it correctly.

At the same time you should use *yourself* as a source of influence. The recognition you give others, the support when things go wrong, the excellent work you produce in your area. It can even be as simple as the way you update your manager on events – via phone, via email, through a weekly update report. None of these require power within the company, but act to build up your own reputation and provide a base for influencing others.

Influencing the boss

Although it seems like your manager holds all the power, there are in fact a number of areas where you can use your influence, unprompted, in a way which will improve your situation. This can include:

- **Providing more than they expected**: Impresses people, improves your reputation, and works on basically everyone, not just your boss.
- **Thinking independently**: Spot problems, think up solutions, assess the political implications, don't throw yourself into stupid ideas, be intelligent, and take the initiative rather than waiting to be told. All of this makes your bosses' life easier, which makes them like you more.
- **Passing on information**: Whether it is information on project status, gossip from the rest of the company, or simply an unbiased report on what is going on. Managers thrive on information flow, so the better you are at delivering, the more valuable you will be.
- **Support**: Support their projects, support them as a team member, and defend them in other meetings and in other groups. This kind of support is noticed by managers (and gossiped to them if they don't) and is highly appreciated – life is difficult when leading, so every bit of support counts.

Typical mistakes

If you aren't used to exerting your influence, then it is likely that you will make a few mistakes at first. This is completely normal and will get better with practice. But before you do reach that point, there are a few typical mistakes which you should keep an eye out for.

- **Not cashing in**: Sometimes you just can't manage to cash in the favours which you've collected. This is often because you are scared of damaging the relationship, don't see the favour as particularly valuable, or don't want to come across as whining. In these situations it's important to open a discussion with other people, to really point out that you are helping them and ask if they see it the same way. Sometimes this will jolt them into helping you of their own accord, sometimes you need to explicitly ask for what you want. But you will never get anything if you don't start talking about it.

Influencing others

- **Framing things as a personal benefit**: It's perfectly fine to want something because it will be good for you. But bluntly asking tends to put people on guard, and they tend to be reluctant with helping you out. Instead, try to frame your requests in a way which make them a benefit to the giver. Everyone likes helping themselves and so this is far more likely to be accepted.
- **Asking before giving**: Things work much, much more easily if you put the effort in and build up some credit with other people *before* you begin making requests.
- **Not being clear**: If you need something, then you need to be clear about what you need. Giving vague hints and suggestions generally leads to help which is imprecise or completely misguided. Particularly in cases where your goal is actually related to the business, clear requests are the way to go.
- **Not emphasising your work**: If you get everything done quickly and without comment, people won't be impressed. If you clearly state how much extra time and frustration the favour cost you, then they start to realise that you are doing them a favour. Never simply say "no problem" to a request, always break down the work and describe what is necessary, and *then* say it can be done.

Tailor your discussion to their personality

What works to persuade one person will not work to persuade another. This is partly based on our needs and wants – if they have no interest in what you can offer, then you (usually) cannot persuade them otherwise. But it is also based on our personalities – what one person finds a convincing argument is a pointless waste of time for another. Thus you should always attempt to match your persuasive style to what you know of your counterparts' personality.

Dominant/pushy personalities

People with a dominant personality enjoy having authority and challenges, they look for prestige and variety in their roles, they want freedom from the decisions of others, and they want the growth and promotion opportunities which will let them reach this point.

When influencing a dominant personality, you should be direct, brief, and to the point – they consider their time valuable, so you should not waste it. Try to follow a few simple approaches:

- Deal with the current situation – ask 'what' is happening, not 'how' it happened.
- Stick to discussing the results they are after, don't waste time on irrelevancies.
- Come prepared with possible options they may follow, emphasise the way that your preferred option helps them obtain more authority or get results.
- Discuss the logical benefits of your idea.
- If you are agreeing on something, then ensure you agree with the facts and ideas rather than the person themselves.
- If a timeline is pressing, then bring this up quickly to emphasise the impact on results and objectives.

Influential personalities

People with 'influencer' personalities look for social recognition and popularity. Their ideal role has people to talk to, comfortable working conditions, and freedom from irritating levels of control or detail-oriented work. They enjoy the chance to motivate people and be included in groups, and look to see their achievements recognised by others.

Influencing these personalities works best in a friendly, social environment. A few pointers include:

- Don't rush – give them a chance to discuss their ideas, other people, and their insights on the matter.
- Provide opportunities or ideas which will help them turn their talk into action and results.
- Show social support for your cause to make it more persuasive – use testimonials from others or mention that the approach has been trialled by other, important groups.
- If you need support to implement a course or program, make sure social activities are built into the schedule.
- Don't focus on the details – you can provide these in a written document or summary, but your discussion should stay on the more general level.
- Ensure that your relationship and interactions are friendly, allowing both to participate in the discussion.
- Make sure that there is an incentive in place for any risks which they may need to take on.

Compliance personalities

People with 'compliance' personalities are detail-oriented, they focus on processes and plans over freeform approaches. They look for roles with personal autonomy, and those which offer them the chance to plan out projects or tasks carefully in advance. They prefer exact job descriptions and precisely-defined expectations.

Combined, this requires you to have a detail-focused approach to influencing their actions. For example:

- Don't just 'wing it', take the time to prepare your approach beforehand (this applies for all personalities, of course, but it's even more so here).
- Be (mostly) open and straightforward – clearly describe the pros and cons of your idea and the alternatives
- Use data to support your claims. Make sure it is accurate, as it *will* be cross-checked.
- Describe your risk-mitigation measures, provide assurance that no surprises will occur.
- Be very precise in your request and the associated tasks, and clearly describe how this will fit into the bigger picture.
- Once you've made your suggestions, recap and summarise everything in a systematic way.
- If you are agreeing on something, then be precise on what you are agreeing to.
- If you disagree, then disagree with the facts, not with the person themselves.
- You will probably have to explain several points, so be ready to do so in a patient and diplomatic way.
- Be persistent.

Steady personalities

These personalities prefer the security of their current situation over the nebulous danger of change. They like to specialise in a specific area with clearly defined limits to their role. When change does happen, it should occur slowly and in a manner which was clearly signposted in advance. They enjoy belonging to a group, and receiving appreciation for their expertise and efforts.

Your approach should focus on meeting their needs for stability. For example, it helps to:

- Ensure that any meeting happens in a set and agreeable environment.
- Show a sincere interest in them as a person, don't appear to be only focused on results.
- Provide answers to 'how' questions, so that they can understand what is happening and why.
- Be patient, ask questions which will draw out their goals and desires.
- If you are changing from the status quo, then present it in a non-threatening way. Give them time during the meeting to take the idea on-board.
- Clearly define the plan, including the respective roles, processes, and their goals.
- Assure them that you will provide support for the entire duration.
- Emphasise that their help and actions will minimise risk and improve current processes – in a safe and well-planned way.

13. Negotiation

Influence is all very well, and it can often bring you very close to your goals without major consequences. But at some stage you will have to deal with a counterpart who doesn't really care about your reasoning. They know what they want, and that doesn't align with your needs. This is where you need to start negotiating.

This is where this chapter comes in. In the following pages, it will cover:

- The basics of negotiating
- Important factors regarding your position which should be determined before you start negotiating
- The first or opening offer
- The bargaining phase of offer and counteroffer
- And the final offer, in which there is agreement or rejection.

Basics of negotiating

In this section we'll look at some of the basics which you should keep in mind before any negotiation, whether it's a friendly chat or a no-holds-barred bloodbath with a political enemy.

Take your time

As a general rule, the one who pushes for the fastest resolution is the one who will have the worse outcome. Settle down, drink your coffee, and take the time to negotiate. The more time and less pressure you have, the more time you can spend on bargaining, offers and counteroffers, and working your way towards a deal which works for you.

'Fair' is a very powerful word

We all want to be dealt with fairly, and we are willing to go to incredible lengths to sabotage a deal if we feel that we have been treated unfairly. Which means that the word 'fair', or the accusation of unfairness, is very, very powerful during a casual negotiation. You can use it in several ways:

- Cast doubt on the reasonableness of your counterpart's offer by saying something like "I just want what is fair".
- Support your own offer and shift attention away from their arguments by noting that "you've made a fair offer".
- Create a feeling of trust and rapport by reassuring your counterpart that you "want them to feel fairly treated".

Don't use 'fair' all of the time, but when carefully planned it can make a very powerful weapon in the emotional battle of a negotiation.

Use leading questions to argue your point

Even in a tense negotiation, people will still instinctively try to solve problems which come their way. You can take advantage of this by using leading questions to push your problem (how you will achieve their terms) over onto your counterparts' shoulders. The trick is to use a question which is open-ended and non-confrontational (which avoids pushback) and which leads the discussion in a direction you wish to follow.

Generally these will begin with 'how' or 'what' – both are non-accusatory and invite further information or help. You can easily take a statement ("do you expect me to cut budget by 30 %?") and rework it into a question format ("how would you suggest I create these budget cuts?"). Some simple examples which work in almost every negotiation are as follows:

- How am I meant to do that?
- What is the biggest problem you have here?
- What is the core issue here?
- How can I help to improve things?
- How would you like me to go ahead?
- What brought us to this state?
- How can we solve the problem?
- What is our objective?

All of these explicitly request help from your counterpart, giving them the feeling of control. It also take a step towards making *your* problems *their* problems – they will now start thinking about how to help you. Which in turn allows you to gently direct the rest of the discussion towards the solution you would prefer.

There are several other sets of questions which you will find handy for identifying stumbling blocks or important information:

- How will this affect the rest of the team?
- What do your colleagues think about this approach?
- What are we up against here?
- What happens if you do nothing?

Negotiation

The last is particularly important, as many people in organisations are quite happy with how things are going, and have no real interest in doing something else (particularly if it makes them look bad). So your job is to make them happy about an upcoming change – and this inevitably revolves around things like status, autonomy, and a fear of looking bad.

Build rapport

People prefer to deal with those they like. And they are willing to extend favourable terms to those they like as well. This is why salesmen try to develop a cheerful personality, and why they spend so much effort making a 'connection' with you – it drives sales. You can use this approach as well.

A negotiation on a tough deadline rarely has time for small talk and biscuits, naturally, but it is always possible to get a little bit of chat in. Introduce yourself, say hi, and spend a few sentences just getting to know each other. Try to make an introductory phone call before the big meeting – this can always be disguised as a discussion on meeting logistics (something which is helpful in its own right). It doesn't have to be much, but even small steps will help build rapport. And this in turn will help you negotiate.

Use active listening

In any conversation there will be time when the other person is talking – this is theoretically the time when you should be listening to what they are saying (duh, right?). Yet many of us use the time to think about *our* next comment, about what we will say next. This is common but foolish.

Focus on your counterpart, listen carefully to what they are saying. Note any difficulties which may be occurring such as frustration or challenges Paraphrase their sentences to ensure and check your level of understanding – this reassures your counterpart that you are paying attention and helps build rapport.

Ask questions

Information is the heart of negotiation, and the one who knows more information is usually in the better position. So try to gain as much as you can – ask your counterpart as many questions as you think you can get away with.

But be careful with *what* you ask. Questions with yes/no answers will only provide specific information, but a chain of them may be used to lead your counterpart to a certain conclusion. Leading questions (e.g. "don't you agree that we should do this?") may gain agreement *in the conversation* but will not lead to agreement afterwards. Open questions (e.g. "can you tell me about the problems with this project?") are better for gathering information, and will avoid your biases from influencing their behaviour.

If you find that one area or discussion point is causing difficulties in the negotiation, it can be worth asking a very targeted question to get more information on the subject. This can help you figure out other offers or compromises to make. For example:

- It seems that you value [X]
- It seems like you don't like [X]
- I feel that you're reluctant to try [X]

Maximise alternatives
We go into the concept of leverage in the next section, but it can basically be summarised as follows: whoever has the better alternative has more power in the negotiation. This is why it is important to maximise the number of alternative options you have *before* starting the negotiation. You will be confident (which improves results) and willing to walk away if you don't get your desired outcome (which improves results). There is literally no downside to have multiple alternative options during a negotiation.

Practice makes perfect
Negotiation is a skill like any other, and as such it needs to be practiced before you will be good at it. But how do you do this? A negotiation is a complex, many-layered thing, and it is difficult to consciously 'practice' while it is going on.

So instead, you should try to practice one phase at a time. Start at the first offer, and try to improve. Then work on your counteroffer skills. And then your closing arguments. The later sections cover a variety of useful tips and strategies for each phase of the negotiation. Many of the examples cover negotiation around money, as budget jockeying is a big part of the manager lifestyle. However you can adapt these techniques to any currency being traded.

Factors to determine before you start
There are several interrelated factors which you need to keep in mind before you go into any negotiation.

Negotiation

- Your **target price** is the goal you are looking to achieve – it's what you would consider a fair offer if selling, and a fair purchase if buying.
- The **bottom line** is the absolute *worst* deal which you could accept doing. Any offer which doesn't meet your bottom line isn't worthwhile, so you are better off walking away.
- The **walk-away option** is *what you will do* if you decide not to continue negotiating. This is also known as the BATNA, or Best Alternative to a Negotiated Agreement.
- Your **leverage** is how much power you have in the negotiation. Generally, the better your walk-away option, the more leverage you have – this also applies if you have competing offers, more options, or simply don't *need* to make a deal.
- The **negotiating personalities** on each side of the deal, as this will impact how you both push your respective agendas. Generally you will be dealing with analytical, accommodating, or aggressive negotiators.
- The **decision-maker** is the person who will actually say 'yes' to a deal in the end. The **decision-killer** is the person (or more often, people) who do not *decide*, but whose negative impression can stop the process dead.

These are complex, and will be covered in more detail in the following sections.

Target price

You (hopefully) have an idea of the value of the thing you are negotiating over. It might be a budget cut, a project funding request, a sale, it doesn't really matter. The important thing is that you know what you would offer or accept as a 'fair' price in your particular situation. Naturally you will try to get a better offer than this, but this gives you an idea of where to aim for.

As part of your preparation, you should think through best-case and worst-case scenarios. Worst-case is obviously the very edge of what you would accept. Best-case is what you could hope for, but keep in mind that the real outcome may be even better than you expected. Be flexible, particularly when it comes to winning!

The number you take into the negotiation, at the front of your mind, should be your *best-case* option. Try not to spend too much time worrying about your bottom line, and do not highlight this number in any notes you bring into the negotiation. This is a minor psychological trick which causes you to focus on that number during stressful situations (i.e. negotiations). Rather than focusing on a lower number (the bottom line) you force your attention onto a higher one and anything less than that seems like a loss. We hate losing, so this has a knock-on effect on your overall success rate.

Bottom line

The bottom line is the worst possible option which you would accept in a negotiation – it's not a successful deal, or a good one, but it's an *acceptable* deal. Identifying this point is essential for determining your negotiation strategy, and keeping it clear in your mind will prevent you from jumping at a bad deal in the heat of negotiation.

This is not to say that the bottom line is an inflexible barrier. Sometimes you may have an unreasonable number in your head, one which simply won't fly in the real world. You may need to adjust it as other factors and currencies enter the negotiation, particularly if you think you can get more valuable concessions from the other side. Telling yourself that your bottom line is unchangeable robs you of the flexibility which you might need to find the best outcome for you. Think of it as a (firm) guideline for your negotiation, not a rule.

Walk-away option

Sometimes negotiations simply don't work out, and you have to walk away. The walk-away option, or BATNA (Best Alternative to a Negotiated Agreement) is what you will do instead of going on with the negotiation. You accept that there won't be an agreement, and so decide to go elsewhere. Perhaps you look for support from another manager, you scrounge budget savings from somewhere else, you fire half the team. Whatever it is, it's not a negotiation.

This of course is difficult, because after a few rounds you are normally quite invested in the negotiation and just want the damn thing to go ahead. It's also difficult when you don't have many other options, or if the outcome is important for you. Which is why it's important to have multiple different options open for achieving your goals. Even if you've only thought about it, just *knowing* that this is not your only option makes you much more confident in your negotiation. Which in turn makes you a tougher negotiator, which in turn leads to better outcomes.

Negotiation

Leverage

Leverage is the amount of power which you have to push your counterpart's decisions or actions. It can lie with either side of the negotiation (often on both sides), and it can be split into positive, negative, and moral leverage:

- **Positive leverage** is the ability to provide or withhold something which your counterpart wants, be it a successful project, a sale to the business, etc. Positive leverage is very useful as it increases the desire on both sides to reach a deal – the famous 'win-win' situation.
- **Negative leverage** is the ability to make your counterpart suffer, by reducing their power, embarrassing them, taking away the Christmas bonus, etc. To use this effectively, you need to understand what is most important to your counterpart, and determine how you can threaten that. However, you should never *directly* threaten someone, this is often seen as an attack on autonomy and will trigger an irrational response, often one which kills the entire negotiation. Instead, label the leverage without going into detail ("it seems you value your Christmas bonus") – let them figure out the consequences themselves.
- **Moral leverage** is the difference between what your counterpart *believes* and how they are *acting*. Few people like to look like hypocrites, so if you can show that they are acting inconsistently then you can push them towards a desired action. Doing this effectively requires you to carefully listen to what they are saying and how they are saying it, using it to build a map of their beliefs.

The success of negotiation often depends on the power of the leverage available for each side. There are three situations which you will find yourself in:

- **Your options are better**: You don't need their help as much as they need yours, you are happier to walk away than they are. This provides you with leverage, and allows you to push the negotiation further than otherwise possible. Even in this situation, your opponent will push for any advantage they can get – it's important to remember that you have the stronger position and so don't need to bargain with them. Just say no to their requests, or demand higher concessions.

- **Their options are better**: They have the upper hand and are using it to demand concessions from you. You need to push back to try and eke out every advantage you can, while trying to diminish or nullify their leverage. The mental game comes in here, many people *think* that they are in the weaker position, but an objective observer would rate both sides as equal. Your mental image of your leverage is very important for your willingness to negotiate.
- **Both options are terrible**: Sometimes neither side can walk away without ruining everything. This is an interdependent relationship, and one where you really have to aim for a win-win bargain. Any sort of hard negotiating here tends to screw you both over, if not now then in the future.

Remember that leverage is as much felt as measured – you can often make your counterpart believe you have a strong position by confidence and hard negotiation, even when you have nothing to fall back on. This is, of course, a bluff (or at least a strong exaggeration), which means that you will have many problems when the bluff is finally called. Bluffing is particularly obvious when people threaten to 'walk away' from a deal if they don't get their way – this is a common tactic and one which you can almost always ignore.

The negotiation personalities involved

We all have a baseline personality, one which we feel most comfortable using in our daily interactions with others. It's not always the same, we vary it depending on the situation and the circumstances, but we tend to fall back to our 'standard' personality in stressful situations, such as tough negotiations. As a rough rule of thumb, we all fall under three main groups – analytical, accommodating, and aggressive – and this also applies to those we are negotiating against.

Analytical

Analytical negotiators focus on details and preparation, they prepare for any situation which may occur prior to the negotiation and consider that it is better to spend more time and be more successful. They tend to be reserved personalities, enjoy problem-solving, and are very invested in the idea of 'fair' trades for their concessions. They will happily take time to reassess the latest counter-offer to determine how it fits into their analytical model.

If *they* are analytical types, then your best hope at carrying an argument is through liberal use of facts and data. Don't surprise them with new information, as this will trigger another round of analytics, instead flag issues early and clearly. If they are silent, then they are probably assessing what you have just said. Don't keep talking, let the silence go on.

If *you* are an analytical type, then you will have a strong set of information going into the negotiation. But you should work on strengthening the rapport with your counterpart – smile, chat, and be interested in their needs.

Accommodating

Accommodating negotiators are most interested in the relationship between the two counter-parties. They will focus on communication and win-win objectives, even if this is not actually necessary. They tend to be very friendly and willing to give concessions in the name of keeping the negotiation 'personable' – hoping that this will be returned by their counterparts in time. This may lead them to offer things which simply aren't possible.

If *they* are an accommodating type, then you should embrace the small chit-chat and relationship building, but keep nudging them towards concrete actions and commitments. You will need to be careful when dealing with areas of potential disagreement, as an accommodating person will tend to avoid discussing these in favour of happier topics.

If *you* are accommodating, you should keep up with your likeable approach (as this is always a bonus), but don't go overboard into pointless discussion and time-wasting. Keep a firm eye on the problem points of the deal and don't be afraid to bring them up – even if this will cause some conflict.

Aggressive

Aggressive negotiators like winning, regardless of the impact on long-term business or personal relationships. They focus on the now, and prefer to have a *closed* deal rather than a *perfect* deal. They will tend to ignore other opinions or comments until they have said what they want to say.

If *they* are an aggressive negotiator, then you should allow them to tell you their entire opinion – only after this will you be able to say anything yourself. Use repetition and open-ended questions to get more information out of them, use a summary of their statements to get that initial agreement. This is the point where you can start to negotiate back. Concessions are usually a waste of time, aggressive negotiators will simply accept them and keep pushing.

If *you* are an aggressive negotiator, then your tone of voice and pushy attitude will tend to put others off. This may not affect the current deal, but will affect those in future. Back off slightly, deliberately cultivate a friendly tone to build rapport with your counterparts.

Decision-makers and decision-killers

There are two very important groups of people in any negotiation, and these are not necessarily involved in the negotiation. They are the **decision-makers** and the **decision-killers**, and it is vital that you identify who they are if you want to make any real progress.

- The **decision-maker** is the one who will *approve* the final deal. Note that is not the one who is part of the negotiation, but the one who will say, after various discussions, that this deal is acceptable to the company, department, etc. If you are dealing with larger projects, this will often be a member of upper management with direct budget responsibility (the one with the money has the final say, after all). They will often have their own interests which are separate from the project itself – managing to appeal to these needs will often boost your chances of a deal, even if it doesn't seem to work on the surface.
- The **decision-killer** is anyone who has the ability to block a deal from happening, even if it has been approved. This usually someone directly impacted by the outcome and who is on a decision-making governance board or who has a close relationship to the decision-maker themselves. These are most obvious when a deal will lead to a loss of power/prestige/money in a certain department, and you will need to find a way to keep them happy to get it through. The usual approach is to provide something nice to the decision-killer themselves, so they feel better about the hit their group is about to take. Keep the various currencies in mind to identify those which may work here.

The first offer

Negotiations invariably start with one side or another making a first offer – whether it's the car salesman noting his asking price or the manager demanding you decrease headcount by 30%. This is a key moment because it marks the point at which *negotiation* begins, rather than just jockeying for position.

Negotiation

The first offer sets the stage for all the bargaining later on. If you think of the first offer as the wish, and the best-and-final offer as the lowest you can possibly go, then everything between there is potential profit which you can grab. Which means that you need to have a strong opening position to improve your chances through the entire negotiation.

How do you do this? Get them on the defensive, be deliberate and thoughtful, and challenge their tactics. Here are a few approaches which will be covered in more detail in the following sections:

- Never make the first move.
- Make them defend their number.
- Place a conditional first offer.
- Your offer is the correct one, because…

Never make the first move

Tough negotiators will usually try to put you on the defensive right from the start of the negotiation. You will frequently hear a statement along the lines of 'you need my help more than I need yours', 'I have plenty of other people I could be working with', or 'didn't I give you a lot of support in the last project?' All of these are designed to make you feel that you have less power in the relationship, which will in turn push you to make more concessions. This is where it helps to have a thick skin, as you need to ignore the meaning of these statements while simultaneously negating them. Responding in a polite, calm way (e.g. 'actually, 'need' is an overstatement, we are equals after all') will help you start out on an even footing.

Once all of this petty manoeuvring is out of the way (for the moment at least), it's time to get the first offers out in the open. Your initial offer should be based on your leverage in the deal – in other words, do you have something which is considered rare or otherwise valuable by your counterpart? Or are you offering vague promises and uninteresting rewards? This affects how much you can ask for and how hard you can bargain.

You are *almost always* better off if your counterpart makes the first offer. This gives you an idea of how far apart your estimates are, and thus whether you should be asking for more or less than you planned. Preferably more, obviously. Here are a few generic questions which may help you get their initial position out in the open:

- "Is this already budgeted? Can you share the number?"

- "Do you have a number in mind? Can you give me an idea what that is?"
- "Can you give me a ballpark figure to begin with?"
- "What do you think this opportunity is worth?"
- "Do you have an idea of the approximate cost?"
- "Is there a number (cost, FTEs, etc.) you are trying to stay under (or over)?"
- "When you had a similar project in the past, what did you need?"
- "How long have you had this system? Can you tell me how much it required originally?"
- "Can you tell me what other departments are proposing?"

This is, naturally, not easy – your counterpart will also be trying to force you into making the first move. You will need to defend yourself with a more-sophisticated version of saying 'I asked you first' – respond with a comment about not really knowing what the value should be, then ask for their help. Appear vague and perhaps a bit naive, but prepare to jump on anything which they say in return. You may also try offering a very high (or low) value which someone else would require – i.e. "company X would charge $3k per day for this one". This acts as an initial offer without actually being an initial offer.

The only thing to be careful of when doing this is the so-called 'anchoring bias', in which the first number which is mentioned will subconsciously influence the rest of the negotiation. Throwing out a ridiculously high (or low) number to start the bargaining will tend to drag all following counters in that direction, regardless of how ridiculous it appears on the surface. Staying rational after an anchor can be quite difficult, so it helps to either:

- Go on the attack immediately by forcing them to defend the feasibility or reality of their position ("How did you come up with that number?", "How am I meant to do that?")
- Deflect the discussion onto the end goal of having a deal rather than the compromises needed to reach this ("What are we trying to achieve together here?")
- Push for an immediate concession from their side, but target another factor which you are discussing ("What else could you offer to make that a good price?")

Negotiation

Anchoring also exists on the emotional level, an opponent may go on and on about how terrible their upcoming offer will be, then give a slightly-less terrible actual offer. As you are primed to expect something bad, the new offer is better than expected and thus appears to be reasonable. Both of these anchoring biases are dangerous for your negotiation, and you thus need to stay alert for their impact. Keep your target number in mind to minimise this impact, and then challenge their initial offer to force the anchor from its initial position.

Make them defend their number

First offers are often wildly high or low, just to set the stage for further negotiation. It is rare to find an initial number which has been well thought out and planned, and you can use this to your advantage right from the start of the negotiation. Challenge their offer and ask them to defend where it came from. Very few people bother to do this during negotiations, so you will usually catch your counterpart off-guard.

How do you do this? Here are a few sample questions which you can throw into the mix:

- How did you come up with that number?
- That's odd, why did you start with such a high (or low) amount?
- I don't understand the logic of that one, can you explain the reasoning behind it?
- That seems like a large ask, can you tell me what it's based on?

You should also push to see how flexible they are when it comes to negotiating that offer. Simply ask how fixed their needs are, or if they have room to compromise on different factors. Note that *whatever* they say, you will still be able to negotiate (albeit with more effort) – but you get the idea of accepting compromise into their heads from an early stage. Some people will even drop a requirement or two immediately, just in response to being asked.

Place a conditional first offer

Now that you've heard their first offer, was your planned offer too low or too high? Is their position weakly justified? Then revise your initial number to take advantage of this. It often helps to throw out your own wildly-ridiculous starting offer, this acts as a counter-anchor to their starting offer and thus helps balance the field. A good rule of thumb is to offer around 65% of your target price (if buying) or 155% (if selling).

An easy trick to add to the believability of your number is to make it a slightly odd one. A budget request of $100,000 looks like you're making it up, but a request of $108,500 looks like some calculation has gone into it. It seems more "serious", and thus is more likely to persuade your counterpart.

Naturally this assumes that you know what your offer should be, roughly, and are able to revise it in a reasonable way. In other words, don't change your planned starting point by too much, because once you've announced your number then you will inevitably be challenged in return.

"Is this price firm or negotiable?" they will ask. The answer is neither. The price is the *correct* one.

Your offer is the correct one, because

Any offer you put on the table is immediately open to attack by your counterpart. They may say that you are asking for too many resources for the financial year, that you want too many people to complete the project, or that you are asking for too high a salary. Management or HR will inevitably 'challenge' numbers which they don't like the sound of, often simply because they can.

In this situation, many people will immediately propose a reduced offer – particularly when they feel pressure to make the deal or get the agreement. This is inevitably a bad idea, you will lose ground in negotiation for no real reason at all. Instead, you should *defend* your offer. Simply start by saying that it is a fair and reasonable offer, and then go on to explain why this is.

Naturally, this assumes that you have a strong reason as to why your offer is a correct one. And that you are capable of explaining this, logically, confidently and calmly, to your opponent. The main questions which you will (inevitably) need to cover are "how did you arrive at this requirement?" and "why should I provide it?"

If you cannot do this, right now, *before* going into negotiations, then you should spend some time thinking about your approach. The second question is particularly important, as it allows you to tie any request into the overall benefit of the person or company as a whole – which is often the only way to get your target. Many offers are difficult to defend as they are (you may really be asking for too many people, for example), but can be defended by showing that the extra headcount will allow you to provide additional features and thus additional value to the company.

Be creative and flexible, as a good justification leads into a stronger initial position, while placing your opponent on the defensive. Ensure that you emphasise the special benefits which *only* you or your offer can provide. This avoids your counterpart treating you as a 'commodity', which leads them to compare your offer to what others can provide and so creates a race to the bottom.

This doesn't mean you will get what you ask for, of course, but it does set you up for the next stage.

Offer and counteroffer

Once both initial offers are on the table, it's time to move on to bargaining. Despite a common belief that the best negotiator doesn't move from their initial offer, a well-planned set of concessions from your initial position is often the only way to get a deal done. Having a well-researched initial offer (and casting doubt on theirs) is a good way to keep the final outcome closer to your target, but you have to accept that you cannot always get everything you ask for.

Which is where bargaining comes in. Many people hate negotiation, they feel dirty haggling and simply want to get it over with. This is what your counterpart is looking for, as it inevitably means a better deal for them. Roll your sleeves up and get stuck into the tough and sometimes nasty offer and counteroffer – after a while you will begin to enjoy the challenge, and this will make you far more successful in your eventual outcomes.

But how do you actually do this? It can be difficult to be assertive in a negotiation, particularly if you don't have an aggressive personality at heart. There are a couple of approaches which are quite helpful in this regard, as described below. But remember that being assertive is not the same as making enemies. Your counterpart is not the enemy, the issue you are dealing with is the problem.

- **Get strategically irritated**: Anger makes us do stupid things, but controlled, visible anger is a powerful indicator to your counterpart that you are not happy with their proposal. If you have a bad offer, a really irritating one, then allow a little bit of this irritation to come through in your voice as you say "I cannot see how that would ever work." Your counterpart will often back off on the point, often sub-consciously.

- **Be icily controlled**: If your negotiating style so far has been open and friendly, then a sudden switch to a controlled, poised, and *confident* tone of voice is also a clear sign for your counterpart. Be calm, be confident, and say "that doesn't work for me".
- **Ask why**: Whenever someone asks 'why', we automatically go on the defensive. You can use this to express your dissatisfaction ("why do you think that would be appropriate?") or to try and trigger more concessions ("why would my boss agree to this deal?").

During the offer/counteroffer stage, both sides move away from their initial positions and slowly converge on an acceptable mid-point. There are many different decisions which need to be made here, particularly involving how much you are willing to give up and what you will demand in return. But if done well, you can significantly improve the final outcome.

Any negotiation involves a give and take exchange. But you should always remember to *trade* concessions. *Never* give something up without demanding something in return. Importantly, you should get something concrete in return – never give something up in the hopes of gaining 'goodwill' from your counterpart. A tough negotiator (i.e. everyone above middle management) will simply take the unexpected bonus and continue to play hardball as before.

Concessions can be almost everything, even if the main topic you are negotiating is cash related (i.e. usually budget or headcount). You can make changes to what you are promising to do (deadlines, scope, etc.) or move into the currencies which are specific to your counterparts wants (political support, access to new information, etc.). Anything you can think of may be used as a bargaining chip in this phase of the negotiation, and so it helps to be a bit creative and think of ideas beforehand.

This of course brings up the two big questions – how much should you concede, and how much should you ask for in return?

Particularly in the first counteroffer, you should be careful not to go too far from your initial offer, as this will give the impression that you were simply lying to start with. This impression damages trust and will make them less flexible for the reminder of the bargaining. By contrast, a truly minor concession just seems unreasonable, which has the same effect. So aim to offer a 'reasonable' concession, though naturally what this actually is depends on your negotiation. If you followed the earlier approach of offering 65% of target price as an initial offer, then a nice rule of thumb is to calculate several increments of 85% and 95% of your target price. Be sure to fudge the numbers a bit so they seem exact rather than round ($3521, not $3500) as this boosts credibility.

What you should ask for is another difficult question. If your concession has a calculable value (reduction in headcount required for a project, for example) then you should ask for something with a similar value to it (all bonuses are increased by X% if it is completed on time). If there is no real number which you can assign to your concession, then try to get as much as you can.

Easy, right? Not at all, this is one of the hardest parts of negotiation. Here are a few areas to work on, which again are described in more detail in the following sections:

- Never just agree.
- Always trade concessions.
- Trade things which are cheap to you, but valuable to them.
- Challenge counteroffers.

Never just agree

If your counterpart asks for a concession, *never, ever* say 'sure, we can do that'. Even if you can do it. Nothing is ever free, it is always worth something.

'Free' is also a word which you should be careful to avoid. Every time you make a concession, it should feel like a concession – you are clearly and obviously helping your counterpart out. Make a big deal out of everything you do for them. It will make you look like you're caving, even when you aren't. Even if something is free for you and can be offered free, don't tell them. Everything has a cost – even if that cost is only to you and the additional efforts you will need to do. They won't know this by themselves, so make it clear! "Yes, I can do that project without any extra help from you, *but* I will need to deal with other managers whose projects will be delayed. I am willing to do that for you to further our working relationship".

This type of comment changes a 'yes, of course' concession into one which clearly shows the effort you are putting in.

Any concession you make should be made as dramatic as possible. This reduction in headcount risks project success, moving the deadline forward by a month will require scope changes (even if there is plenty of slack time). You get the idea. Don't lie, as this will cause problems when you are inevitably found out, but make it sound difficult. Then ask what they can offer to help you get past this problem. Say you can do it, but not with your current headcount. Or not while doing your other tasks. Do this as a first step towards trading concessions.

Some handy phrases here include:

- "That's a big ask, I'm not sure we have available capacity."
- "Are you being serious?"
- "I might be able to get it done, but not with the current set-up."

Always trade concessions

One typical mistake bad negotiators make is to move further and further from their initial position without asking for anything in return. Whenever your counterpart asks for something, you should first ask yourself if you need to make a concession at all. Are you the only one that can do this? Essentially irreplaceable? Politically powerful? Then you may have the leverage to simply refuse any change to your deal.

Assuming you can't just reject the concession, you should next ask if you can offer a reduced version. If you should reduce headcount by 10%, ask for 7%. Their request should be considered a starting position for bargaining – the worst they can say is 'no'.

The last question to ask is what you can get in return for this concession. Any deal has a number of different factors, and all of them may be put on the table as part of the trade. You may need four additional team-members to get the new project done, but will accept their offer of three if you can also pass some uninteresting tasks onto another group. Be strategic and flexible.

Ideally the 'value' of the paired concessions will be equivalent, anything different implies that you're getting a bad deal. If you aren't quite sure what you should value a concession as, try getting them to tell you – simply ask what they think it is worth. Bad negotiators will often tell you what they would give up in return for that concession, and it is often more than you would have asked for.

This will also happen to you, of course, and a typical comment from management is to say that the current plan won't work, so go back and re-assess your forecasts. With no further information, you will go away and miraculously find savings in budget or timelines, which will inevitably blow up in your face when they turn out to be unrealistic. Don't fall for it – ask for more specifics and information on *what* the plan is lacking. Nag if necessary, but make sure you know what value you are aiming for.

Trade things which are cheap to you, but valuable to them
As mentioned above, there are normally many different factors which may be in play in any negotiation. This includes the usual ones (headcount, budget, etc.) but also the numerous 'currencies' which are described in a previous section (see here for more details). Once you have figured out the factors which 'could' be negotiated, then you need to determine how they relate to each other

You should know which factors are most important to you (and thus must be protected) and which are most important to your counterpart (and thus may be worth trading). Be careful when you do this assessment, because seemingly 'small' factors can have a large impact on overall outcomes. Think it through a couple of times before you take any action.

This of course leads directly into your counteroffer. Feel free to make concessions on factors which are unimportant for you, but significant for the other side. If you can provide political support or space on a high-profile project, trading for a solution to your current problem, then go ahead and offer it.

Challenge counteroffers
Just as you challenged the initial offer, feel free to challenge their counteroffer as well. Ask them how they arrived at this suggestion, suggest that their numbers aren't based in logic or reality. Ask if there is flexibility in this proposal, or why they believe that their proposal is reasonable given the current circumstances. All of the approaches from the initial offer can be reused again here.

Why bother? It keeps your counterpart on the defensive and breaks up their rhythm. It also makes it clear that you will challenge anything they say, which forces them to carefully plan any counteroffer before it is made. Any additional difficulty you can place on your counterpart will help your overall negotiation success.

The best and final offer

Eventually one person will run out of things which can be traded, or simply run out of interest in continuing the negotiation. You may have a good position, or a mediocre one, and you're probably tired of arguing about little details. But you still need to suck it up and continue through to the end, because many excellent negotiation positions have been lost at the last minute by a failure to hold ground.

This is partly due to those last minute 'oh, and just one more thing' comments which your counterpart will make. And partly it is due to our habit of just 'wanting to get it over with' and so adding extra concessions to get a fast deal. This is inevitably a worse deal than if you were persistent – the faster the negotiation is wrapped up, the more likely you missed out on something.

This is where the 'best and final offer' comes in, the statement that it is either (a) accept this, or (b) walk away. There should be no counter-offers at this point, it's just 'we have a deal' or not. At least in theory. Although it sounds simple, there is often a constant pressure to make tiny little concessions even at this stage – something which can significantly decrease your final outcome. You will also find that the longer you are engaged in a negotiation, the less likely you are to walk away. The hours of time sunk into haggling are seen as 'wasted' if you don't follow through, and tough negotiators will take advantage of this.

It is thus important to keep your bottom line, walk-away option, and leverage in mind here. The bottom line and walk away let you decide when negotiation is worthwhile, and leverage lets you decide how hard to push.

Sounds complicated, right? So what do you do? Here are some main tactics to use:

- Evaluate both sides' walk-away options.
- Be the first to ask for a final offer.
- Always counter the final offer.
- Never let them counter your final offer.

Negotiation

Evaluate both sides' walk-away options

Just as you have a walk-away option, so does your counterpart. Successful negotiation, particularly at the end stage, is a matter of understanding just what options each side has. This directly ties into the concept of leverage which we discussed at the start of the chapter. If you appear to have a stronger set of alternatives to the negotiation, then you have more power to push for concessions.

The important word here is 'appear'. You will never have full knowledge of your counterparts' situation, and they have the same problem with you. Thus even in situations where you have no good alternatives, *appearing* to have a strong position will help you through the negotiation.

At the same time, you need to decide if your counterpart has a strong position or not. Ignore how they act and look at the facts you have in hand – are they under pressure from another source? Do they have a *plausible* alternative to dealing with you? Is your assistance required or are they just bargaining to see where it goes? All of this information helps determine their position, which in turn lets you decide how far to push.

Be the first to ask for a final offer

As negotiation goes on, you'll realise that your counterpart is running out of concessions to make. Generally the first counteroffer has the biggest concession, then each subsequent one will make smaller and smaller concessions as they get closer and closer to their bottom line. There will also be a longer and longer gap between counteroffers, as the discussion about what can still be offered gets more and more difficult.

There is no real rule for the number of offer/counteroffer rounds which will occur. Complex and valuable trades have more, cheap and simple have less. It's up to you to determine when your counterpart is getting closer to their bottom line, that you have pushed them as far as they will go. Then ask for their final offer. Being first to do so keeps your counterpart off guard and avoids giving further concession away.

Always counter the final offer

Once you've finally gotten their final offer, then it's time to try and counter this offer. You should never miss a chance to try and get one last bit of value out of the deal. Ask for 'just one more thing', say the deal would be perfect if there was just a tiny change. And then once they give you that one more thing, then counter that concession as well. Does it make you a bit of a dick? Yes, but this slow process of eroding their position will lead to a steady improvement in yours.

Of course, you don't want to get greedy and jeopardise the entire deal. There's a simple way of deciding what to ask for here:

- Does the current offer work for you? If yes, ask for 'just one more little thing', sell it as a minor change. If they push back or look like they will pull out of the deal, drop the request and go back to the previous final offer.
- If the current offer isn't acceptable for you in its current state, then make a complete counteroffer with new concessions. If they consider the counter, then you keep negotiating and end up somewhere better. If they say no, then you walk away with minimal loss.

Asking for a minor thing can add up over time, particularly if you're dealing with large numbers. You may not get what you ask for, but it never hurts to try.

Never let them counter your final offer

The reverse applies if you make a final offer. Once it's made, it's made, and it should never be modified. Your final offer is (in theory at least) the point at which you are willing to walk away rather than bargain further.

This is the theory, at least. In reality there is always pressure to make just one more concession, and you will often be asked if this is your best, final offer. This is a difficult question. If it's *not* your best offer, saying 'yes' may lose you the entire deal. Saying 'no' at this point will simply encourage them to ask for more. So instead, use the moment to trade more concessions from your counterpart. If asked, simply say that this is best deal you can do *at this moment*. But if they have *something else* to add to the mix, it could be considered. This puts the focus back on your counterpart, and they will often open the negotiation up again in a way which allows you to get more concessions.

If it *is* your best offer, then that's it. You have to be willing to accept losing a deal at this point, because this is (theoretically) the end of the negotiation – it's now just 'yes' or 'no'. In practice you will inevitably be asked for just one more concession, which you can either ignore ('no, that's my final offer') or trade further if you truly feel there is no other option ('this could be acceptable, but I would need…')

14. Risky situations

Talent at office politics is a great thing to have, but sometimes you find yourself in a situation which is *dangerous*. In other words, the outcome may lead to you having major setbacks to your career, or even losing your job entirely. In these situations you need to be sure that you are flexible, that you at least try one last time to win, and that you cover your arse for the inevitable moment when things go wrong.

Be flexible

One of the most useful traits to have in a risky situation is that of flexibility. You presumably have a goal in mind for this situation – it can range from 'successfully solve this problem' through to 'get out with reputation intact'. And you probably planned out a set of steps to achieve this goal. But now things are going crazy and you aren't sure that your plan is relevant at all any more.

This is where flexibility comes in. Are you certain that the previous plan was the only way to achieve your goal? That there are no other possible approaches which you could be taking instead? Is this even the only goal you could be trying for? Could you aim for something more ambitious, less defensive, or perhaps even more defensive and restrained? It is rare that there is only one possible goal and one possible way of achieving it, which means that you can look for approaches which suit your current situation.

Flexibility in planning is a matter of focusing on your ultimate aims rather than the immediate situation. Think about what you want *long-term*, and how the outcomes of this current situation could play into that. Then use this as the basis to hypothesise different outcomes, different approaches, and how you might be able to achieve them. Does this require a lot of effort and brainpower? Yes. But if you want to succeed by more than blind luck, then you need to put the work in.

Try one last push for success

Although this are going downhill, there is still the chance that you can get things to turn around and succeed with the project. Naturally, you want to come out as the main driver of this heroic reversal, but this means you have to be clearly in the middle, pushing for success. So how do you get a stubborn project team to succeed despite themselves? Well…it's hard.

Risky situations

Force action by triggering loss aversion

Let's assume for the moment that you have a good idea of how to solve the current situation, but you cannot get the other stakeholders to agree with you. Discussions and attempts to persuade have not worked out and you are running out of influence to achieve your goals.

In these situations, it can be worth deliberately triggering loss aversion in your counterparts. Loss aversion is the innate dislike which we all have to losing something – we would rather bet everything on the chance of winning than take a smaller, yet certain loss. This is consistent across organisations and cultures and is one of the main reasons why department programs survive far longer than they should – no-one wants to accept the loss of the resources invested to date.

Luckily we can also use this tendency to get others interested in the project again. By triggering the innate sense of loss aversion in your counterpart, you can get responses and help from those who have spent weeks ignoring your emails and calls.

Here are some basic questions which you can include in your discussion, it's rarely necessary to go into more detail:

- As I have not heard from you, I assume your priorities have changed. As such I will move to close down the project.
- Have you given up on settling this topic amicably?
- Have you accepted that you will not receive any benefit from this project?

Sprinkle these into your conversation or send a simple email with just one of them. You will be surprised how quickly you get a response.

Just take action

It is certainly possible to argue with people until they agree with your approach. This is rarely a long-term solution, they will remain irritated at you for far longer than the disagreement could possibly warrant. Instead, change people's minds by *doing* – simply go ahead and do your preferred action and let them follow along.

This requires that your approach be the best one, naturally. If this is the case, then you can happily point to the successful outcomes and claim that you were responsible for the improvements – trumpet this loudly to management and peers, quietly noting that the other approach would never have worked. If your choice turns out to be the wrong one, then blame failure on those that opposed your idea. You *would* have succeeded if not for their doubts and unwanted compromises.

Be secretive regarding your goals
As we've mentioned before, people are always talking about others – this is the cornerstone of society and the basis of office politics. This means that they will also be talking about you, your actions and your words. Try to ensure that you speak with discipline, that you know what you're saying and don't just blather on.

Similarly, you need to be careful that your words aren't seen as empty boasts or promises, there should always be something real behind everything you say. This is not to say that you shouldn't lie, but more that everyone needs a core of truth behind every statement. People you deal with often (which in an office environment is basically everyone) will soon realise that you cannot be trusted and this knowledge will rapidly spread through the organisation.

In the world of office politics, someone will always be plotting. They may have plans to use you as a stepping stone in their career, to block your pet project, to stop your inevitable rise through the ranks. You should be plotting as well, planning out your goals and the actions you need to take. But you should plot in silence, without letting anyone know your goals.

An openly-known goal can be blocked, mitigated, a political enemy can find a backdoor in the office political machine to cut down your success before it arises. Do not give them this opportunity. Take actions, yes, but do not explain what you are doing or why. Let others make their guesses, perhaps they will make the wrong ones.

Cover your arse
Assuming that things are going downhill, then eventually someone is going to have to take the blame. If you are involved in the situation in any meaningful way, then your career is also on the line and you should be planning for the mud-slinging to come.

There are a number of ways which you can cover your arse from unwanted fallout.

Risky situations

Save important emails
Everything goes via email these days, even when it shouldn't. Gossip, unsavoury comments, descriptions of unethical acts, even mundane things such as meeting minutes and discussion of far-reaching decisions for the project. You will recognise these emails when you see them. *Keep them stored somewhere.* Preferably in a system which doesn't delete everything after 3 years, as is often the case with email.

Why bother? It is sadly very common for management to 'forget' that they made a decision which turned out to be a complete waste of time and money. The forgetful manager then drops the blame on someone in the project – saving themselves at the expense of the other's career. If this happens to you (and at some stage it will happen to you) then being able to pull out an old email where this was recorded is a job-saving move. It is also very, very fun to see their reaction – and thus worth doing for entertainment purposes if nothing else.

Document meetings and conversations
Email is easy to archive, but the majority of important decisions are taken in meetings or passed on via conversations. How do you ensure that this is also recorded ahead of the inevitable betrayal when things go wrong? Start taking notes.

In general you should be taking notes of any important conversation or meeting, particularly those where decisions are made which will impact your future. Take those notes (which should include the people present and the date) and use it to send a quick 'confirmation email' to the others involved. This doesn't have to be much, just a quick recap of the discussion and outcomes, sent to everyone to confirm that they agree with your next steps. Store this confirmation somewhere and make sure the important ones are backed up *outside* the company system.

By doing this continuously it will become an expected part of your interactions with others, they will no longer find it odd or suspicious. This in turn allows you to document even controversial comments without getting too much pushback, creating a strong position for any later issues or casting of blame.

The corollary to this is that you will often get similar 'confirmation' emails from others. Always, always check that they are correct and in-line with your memory of the discussion. It is very easy to tweak the record when you write the minutes, and if you don't correct it now then you are stuck with their interpretation.

Use consultants

Consultants have a very special place in the world of office politics. Much like nations use hired mercenaries as a way to achieve military goals in a deniable manner, companies can use consultants as a deniable force to implement organisational goals. This is of course not the usual understanding of consultants, who are theoretically there to enhance your organisational capability on an as-needed basis. But consultants are perhaps most useful acting as the figurative whipping boy.

It works like this. You have an idea, but suspect it may not work or will cause serious political backlash when implemented. You hire a supposedly independent consultant to examine the current situation and propose an idea. Coincidentally, this idea happens to be the one you are promoting. If the idea works, you can take credit when the consultant leaves (it was your championing and implementation that really pushed it through, after all). If it fails, then blame them for everything (outsiders simply don't understand our company culture).

Fake busyness

If you can see that the project is going to die, and in a particularly messy way, then it's time to pull out while you are relatively unscathed. This is often very difficult – others will be doing the same, those who truly believe in the project will have too much to do, and they'll be frantically trying to keep the remaining team members on-board. One of the best ways to get out is to have another project, a very important one, which takes up all of your time and effort. This project doesn't need to exist, but you do need to convince others that it does. Hence it is worth faking busyness for a while, filling your calendar with pointless meetings and sending out droning emails. Others will leave you alone, and you will be out of the way when everything collapses.

Deflect attention to the process

One interesting fact of human behaviour is that we will generally ignore larger decisions in favour of lengthy arguments about very minor factors. Anyone who regularly attends department meetings is undoubtedly familiar with this.

Risky situations

Despite the mind-numbing repetition of these arguments, it is an excellent way to deflect attention from a project which is currently having difficulties. If you report a problem in an open and honest fashion, then everyone will discuss the problem and possible solutions. In theory at least, in reality they will spend the time throwing accusations around and blaming you for being the messenger. However, if you report the problem in a slightly incorrect and ambiguous way, in a manner which is not quite the normal, approved approach for describing problems, then suddenly everyone will start arguing about the process which *should have* been used.

The problem itself will be ignored for a surprisingly long time while this process-related discussion goes on. This gives you extra space to find a solution, propose better ideas, or simply find someone to blame for the inevitable failure.

Scapegoat your predecessor

Projects are long-lasting, employment periods are not. In the majority of cases you will not have been around for the starting work of your current project, often you will not be there for the end. All of your decisions and effort are thus constrained by decisions made in the past, just as your current decisions will constrain others in the future.

What does this mean? Any time something goes wrong, you can gleefully blame it on your predecessors' inability to plan correctly – had they done their job right, you might have a chance now. But they didn't, so how are you meant to succeed? Casting accusations in this way can prevent you being the victim of failing projects, as long as you do it correctly.

What does this mean? Incompetent people are fair game for anything, but if your predecessor was very good at their job (i.e. they were promoted out of it) or well-liked then you will have trouble getting the blame to stick. If this happens, look into the other people involved in the project before you – one of them is likely to have been sufficiently involved that you can make them the scapegoat instead. Also keep in mind that this is a defensive approach, you will not improve your reputation by refusing to take responsibility, but you can prevent it being ruined by current events.

15. Moving to a new role

No position lasts forever, and at some stage you will need to move onwards. This may be via promotion, you may quit to take up something better, you may be fired for incompetence or caught up in a round of layoffs. Regardless of the reason, there will be a point where you at looking for change and deciding if you will take a new opportunity.

This chapter covers a few of the more important pointers when deciding when to go and how to get there.

Moving upwards

In general, you aren't going to stay in your position for your entire career (and if you do, you did something wrong along the way). Ideally you will be moving ever-upwards, going to a position with a higher income, more responsibility, or more interesting work. The less-tempting move is a sideways one which lands you in a role with a very fancy-sounding title, but no actual power. This is basically a nice way of being fired, and so you should take the hint and begin looking for a new position.

Promotion to higher positions or roles with more responsibility are great opportunities, but also great challenges. You will need to carefully assess the new position before you accept – don't jump blindly into taking a job because it looks good. In other words, you should clearly be able to answer the underlying question: *do I really want the promotion?*

There are pluses and minuses to any change, and taking on a higher role is no different. On the **positive** side, you will have a better salary, better recognition, more people to do the mundane work, a stronger chance to really impact company culture or ongoing projects, and increased freedom to do things 'your way'. If you *really* work your way up, then you will find yourself amongst major players in industry and society, regularly interacting with government ministers and generally feeling pretty damn important.

The **negative** side, however, exists as well. You need to be sure that you are capable of performing at this level – no-one should be promoted past the point of their own competence. Higher roles are only effective through the direct actions of their teams, so you will no longer directly affect the outcome of projects. Increased public recognition and dealing with VIPs gets tiring after a while, and requires you to have a happily outgoing personality. The long hours and inevitable relocations also puts significant strain on families and relationships.

As you can see, moving upwards is not always a net positive. The decision to take a promotion is also very dependent on the situation you will be dropping into. Safe situations give you the chance to show success with limited stress, dangerous ones can be high profile successes or failures. Here are the most common situations you will find yourself in:

- **The team was well-run by a competent manager**: The team is likely doing their jobs well, which means that you are unlikely to make a major positive impact. You will regularly be compared to the previous boss. Both of these factors make it difficult to truly stand out and will hurt your chances of being promoted further.
- **The previous manager was terrible but the company is going well**: This gives you an excellent chance to stand out and bring the team up to their required level – something which is almost certain to happen as they are 'pulled up' by the rest of the organisation.
- **The team is great but the company is going badly**: This is a difficult situation, as you will need to be very careful not to be dragged down to the same situation as the others. But any success will look amazing by comparison, making it easy to hop to a higher role in the same company.
- **The team and company are terrible**: You need to look into *why* this is happening. Either the problem is insurmountable and the team is about to be shut down (in which case you should run as far as possible) or you may be able to turn everything around, in which case you will boost your career immensely.

In the end, any decision to move upwards is dependent on the situation. Are you able to manage the workload which is required? Are you able to accept the risks involved, and do you believe that you are able to solve the problems which are present? Think about these carefully before you decide to take a promotion, even if it looks like a dream opportunity.

The interview process

At some stage you are going to be looking for a new job. Ideally you'll find opportunities through your network which will help you move on smoothly (that's one of the big reasons for a network, after all). But if this doesn't work, then you'll be back to the always-annoying process of submitting resumes, talking to recruiters, and doing interviews.

There are no perfect rules or strategies for the interview process, as the needs of the job and the employee required are so varied. Being agreeable and outgoing is naturally a bonus to any job-seeker. Cleverly complimenting the interviewer will work, as long as you are subtle about it. Mirroring their actions is a nice idea but one which usually fails when facing a panel of people – what one interviewer does may be completely at odds with the actions of the others.

In general your best approach is to find out exactly what they are looking for, and then become that person. Use your network, read up on the area, get as much information as you can before the interview, and plan your entire delivery around being the candidate that they want to see.

Beyond this, there are a few tips which may help during the interview process:

- You are a talented, intelligent person who will use their drive and ability to make decisions to solve business problems without the constant supervision of your manager. Sell this fact to them. Once you get past the initial grunt positions, it's assumed that you will be thinking for yourself and taking responsibility – which is why you must be clear that yes, you can do that.
- Similarly, you should sell the fact that your success will make them look good. Ask "what does it take to be successful here?" Listen carefully to the response. And then use this information to decide if the job is interesting and how you can make both yourself and your manager look good.
- Be pushy with non-salary terms of employment. If you're being blocked on the salary negotiations, then feel free to bring alternative factors such as (guaranteed) holiday leave into the equation. Sometimes this is worth more to you than the extra pay, in which case it's worth taking. Sometimes it's a factor which you can then take out of play in exchange for a higher baseline salary. Be creative – the more things you can negotiate on, the better your chances.
- Determine what 'success' is defined as at a very early stage, possibly even in the interview itself if you can manage it. This lets you plan your main tasks before you start, and (perhaps more importantly) allows you to determine what *isn't* important for your overall success.

- There are many places which are 'dream' companies, ones where applicants have been dreaming of a job for years and will fight to the death for a chance to work there. As a general rule, whenever people are emotionally attached or drawn to a job, someone will be trying to exploit this to pay them less money (look no further than arts, the music industry, computer gaming, or even veterinary medicine). Apply there by all means, but watch out for the hordes of competition willing to do it for peanuts and 'exposure'.
- Heavy emphasis on hiring and recruiting in the company culture is either a sign that the company is growing rapidly or that turnover is high. If turnover is high, then you should find out *why* everyone is leaving.
- Try to have multiple interviews and applications on the go at any one time. Not only does this give you practice, but you can use any offer as leverage against another one. Play your offers against one another, it's a good way to squeeze a bit more income out.
- If you have a few interviews coming up, then try to go to the *least* interesting company first. Interviewing is a skill like any other, one which you've probably not practiced recently. If you're going to screw up some interview questions, make sure it's with the boring company first.
- Ensure you get some sort of starting bonus and *save* it. Surviving the first 12 months at a new company can be tricky, particularly if something goes wrong (be it your fault or not) – having that buffer lets you ride out any layoffs which may come along.

Negotiating pay and promotion

The money and position you receive from the company is never fixed in stone, it is a matter of negotiation between you, your manager, and HR. How well you negotiate will determine your starting position, which in turn affects all subsequent movement throughout your career. In other words, it pays to put some effort in at this point.

Your first step will be to establish parameters for your negotiation. How valuable are you to the company? Are your skills difficult to replicate, and thus valuable, or are they fairly simple to replace? Do you have deep knowledge in the area, or are you starting new? If you have rare, specialised skills, is your prospective employer actually aware of that fact? And if not, are you planning to tell them? Finally, you need to decide how much you are willing to push – are you willing to take the chance of losing the position during negotiations? If yes, how much risk are you willing to bear?

Similar information is needed when pushing for promotion or a better bonus after being hired. At this point you will normally have some sort of performance metric which you can point to as evidence of your talent. Throw this information around as much as possible to convince others of your quality. It should be noted that higher positions in the organisation rarely have easily defined metrics, instead you are normally rated on team achievements or overall company performance. These are difficult to quantify and easy to argue, which means that your personal performance rating often comes down to 'does my boss like me?'

Negotiation needs to happen *before* the offer is made – before you have a contract to sign, or a letter with your yearly bonus. At this point everything is fixed and you will have significant difficulty pulling off any sort of change. Instead, begin the negotiation earlier in the process – during the interview for new roles, halfway through the year for current ones. This gives you time to make your desires clear and to negotiate with the organisation.

We cover negotiation in detail within another chapter (page 171). With respect to job negotiations, it is critical to have the underlying basis in place before you negotiate: be well thought of by your manager, be perceived as a hard-working success, be committed but not *too* committed to the role, and have time to work out the details.

Starting at the new job
So you've started at the new job. Congratulations! Now is the time to settle in, build your network, impress people, and avoid screwing up. Easy, right?

Unfortunately no. For all the care you put into investigating beforehand, there will always be something unexpected occurring in the first period of your new role. This is the way of the world, and so you need accept that it will occur and be flexible enough to overcome the associated challenges.

There are a few specifics which you should watch out for when starting a new position:

- The first year at a new job is a delicate and critical time. Particularly in small or fast-growing companies, anyone who can't pull their weight will be quickly dropped and replaced by one of the fresh recruits waiting outside the door. Hope for the best, but plan for

- the worst – avoid buying a house or getting into expensive long-term contracts during that first year.
- If you think you'll be dumped after the first year, but still want the job, then start interviewing at other companies. Come to work in a more upmarket suit a couple of times. Let rumours spread that you are looking elsewhere. The fact that other companies are considering you makes you more valuable to your boss (due to the wonder of outside affirmation) and thus boosts your chances of surviving the yearly purge.
- Stay at least one year at the company, ideally two. Anything less than that looks strange to hiring managers, and you'll need a good explanation for why you left. Even worse, most initial resume screening is done by AI bots these days, and they don't care at all about your explanations.
- Avoid mentioning major debts or long-term commitments such as mortgages or leases at work. There are nice bosses out there, but there are also manipulative ones who will use your need for the job to exploit you. Don't give them the chance – keep the information private.

Once you've started in the new role, you'll need to spend some time observing the other employees. As mentioned in the initial chapter, every organisation has its own level of political activity. Spend some time to determine how politically-driven it is, identify where the hidden networks are, who is an insider in the group, and who seems overly successful for their apparent level of work.

While this is going on, ensure that you keep your thoughts to yourself – don't go on rants to say how untrustworthy everyone is, don't point out the blatant political dealing. Do keep working according to your core values – attempts to drastically change to match the organisation will never stick, especially under stress. You should, however, invest effort into building your own network as quickly as possible. During the initial observation phase you should have identified people who are both well-connected and share some of your values. Make friends with them, find shared goals, and create a sense of solidarity that will keep you going in the initial phases. Outside networks or mentors can be very valuable here, they will help keep you sane and provide a much-needed external opinion.

Regardless of how you prepare, you should be happy with the level of office politics going on in your department. A complete mismatch will either lead to stress (if it's too political for you) or downright boredom (if there's too little politics). If it really doesn't suit, then it is often worth shifting roles to find one which fits better – even lateral moves within the company can lead to surprisingly different levels of political backstabbing.

Lay-offs

There are many reasons why a company will trigger job cuts – and often these reasons are completely out of your control. Although you can't stop layoffs from happening, you can at least spot them coming and try to find a backup plan. Generally there are a range of signals, starting with subtle signs when the layoffs are far away and ending with ringing alarm bells when a mass downsizing is about to occur.

Early signs of layoffs

There are a few early signs which you should keep an eye out for:

- **You lose out on exciting projects**: Despite volunteering for new, critical, or exciting projects, they keep going to someone else. Happens a lot? Manager won't really say why? Start to worry.
- **Non-essential items get cut**: Cost savings hit the small things first – the free lunches or coffee disappears, the Christmas party is half the size, little celebrations are cancelled. This is an early sign that the company is hitting financial troubles.
- **New products are postponed**: A company in trouble will cut back on R&D and new product launches, focusing on those which bring in revenue now, rather than in the future.
- **The department or industry is losing importance**: Business is cyclical, and what is important one year may be irrelevant next year. If you realise that your department is being pushed out of decision-making, or that the industry as a whole is going downhill, then you should start worrying.

Layoffs are a definite possibility

When the company really starts having trouble, you'll get some more obvious signs that your job may be at risk:

- **Cost-cutting is on the agenda**: Suddenly all expenses go under the microscope, buying things is a lot more complex, and whatever limit previously existed for approval-free purchases drops

Moving to a new role

dramatically. This is a pretty clear sign that the firm is suffering financial troubles.

- **Mergers and acquisitions**: When a company is acquired or acquires another, there's a good chance that they will 'discover' a number of duplicate positions. Which will naturally be slimmed down to reduce costs. One of those positions may very well be yours.
- **You're kept out of the loop**: This is the more serious version of missing out on new projects – people are actively avoiding giving you information or preventing you from attending meetings. Speak up, get back on distribution lists and back into those meetings, or you will quickly be seen as outside the 'core' group and thus no longer needed.
- **Executives look stressed**: More stressed than usual, in any case. If senior management or department heads are spending a lot of time in private meetings, and avoiding questions about the future, then you should start to worry.
- **Terrible financial results**: Public companies publish their financials each quarter, which gives you an insight into how they're going. A single quarter with bad results isn't too problematic, but consistently missing earnings forecasts is a sign that something is going badly wrong.
- **Hiring freeze**: The company puts a freeze on new hires. This is basically a 'nice' version of downsizing, as management waits for natural attrition (people quitting or transferring) to reduce the workforce. If it doesn't work fast enough, the freeze will then switch to more direct measures.

Here we go...

And finally there are the clamouring alarm bells which say that a layoff is coming, and soon:

- **Executives are leaving**: Upper management has a far better insight into the health of the company than you do. If a number of them are leaving for 'new options', then you should start to wonder why.
- **People talk about restructuring**: This is a nice way of saying 'we will merge some departments and fire a bunch of people'

- **Layoffs have already occurred**: It's rare that there is only one round of layoffs when the company is in trouble. If you manage to survive the first one, then be on the lookup for follow-up firings once management discovers than the company is still bleeding money.
- **Your boss asks for details of your job**: Particularly detailed written descriptions of your tasks and how they are performed. It could be an attempt to write an SOP for the work, but it probably isn't.
- **Long-term planning is postponed**: Meetings which were meant to be about long-term planning are suddenly postponed. As layoff waves tend to change whole departments, it makes no sense to do any planning before the new structure is in place.
- **Conference rooms are booked out**: Suddenly most of the conference rooms are booked out on the same day, across the entire site. If they're careless, you'll even see that HR has booked them.
- **No home office in day X**: If you are told that you absolutely have to be personally present on a certain day, with no working from home, then this is the day that layoffs will occur.
- **The VPN stops working**: IT is often too fast for their own good, and locks you out of the system before you are officially informed.

16. Typical political shenanigans

There are a number of typical manoeuvres that you will see in a standard office-politics environment. Sometimes they will be directed against colleagues, sometimes they will target you, and sometimes you'll do it to other people. Regardless of the source or the target, it is important to understand what is happening and why.

This chapter will look at the most common political shenanigans, the intention behind them, and how you can defend yourself against it. It has been divided into those which happen on a daily basis, those which are somewhat nastier betrayals, and those with the chance of ending your career.

Daily occurrences

This is a selection of political acts which occur on a day-to-day basis. Expect to see many of these throughout your career.

CC'ing management

Email is a standard part of corporate communications, and most of us spend far too much time deleting the piles of useless junk clogging up our inbox. However email is also a very powerful tool for taking a once-private conversation and throwing it open for the world to see. CC'ing management is a way for workers to make an accusation (true or false) which is in *theory* directed at the target, but in reality is aiming to get management involved (or customers, or executives, etc.).

It is usually irrelevant if the accusation is true or false, because the intention is to force pressure onto the opponent. It is also very difficult to clean up, accusations will stick regardless of what is shown later. Which means that both sides will start throwing in more and more accusations, adding more and more people in CC, in an attempt to shift blame and bring in their supporters.

CC'ing management is a typical tactic in large organisations, a very tempting way to get others to assist you without having to confront them directly. Almost everyone has been on the giving or receiving end of it, and it wastes a vast amount of everyone's time.

If you are being targeted

Writing an insulting or nasty reply to the email is very tempting, but this is often what they want you to do. Email is a permanent record, which means anything you write can be used against you – and will. Instead, move to a telephone call or face-to-face meeting – without warning them beforehand. This leaves no permanent record and skips the escalation of the issue. You will also find that those who are brave via email are cowards in person, and you can overwhelm this with a strong display of confidence.

Remember to be calm and collected. Don't get emotional, as this will ruin your credibility. Get your facts and story in line before the meeting, rehearse what you want to say and how you will say it. Then go and speak to your accuser. Feel free to ask a few accusatory questions (what were you hoping to achieve by CC'ing these people? Do you feel it has succeeded? What should we do to avoid this problem in future?). If you are bold enough to confront them, then they will quickly learn not to do it again.

If you are doing this
In general this is a trick which is not worth doing. Your management won't want to be involved (as they expect you to sort out problems by yourself). Their management won't want to be involved for the same reason. It also leaves a very clear trail of who said what, which means that any exaggerations or lies will be traceable. It will work on those who feel guilty or are otherwise easy to push around, but people who are easily pushed around can also be manipulated via positive persuasion.

Deals in the corridor
This is the art of working out deals and support for your positions in the corridor outside the meeting room, rather than the meeting room itself. Perhaps less of a political shenanigan than a basic fact of office life, being able to pull people onto your side before the voting starts is often essential to getting anything done. Which means that you'll need to be comfortable with making deals in the corridor, both as the asker and the listener.

Where this moves into the field of 'nasty tricks' is when people begin coercing others into supporting them – bullying, manipulating, blackmailing, etc. Generally it won't reach this level, but when a truly important deal is on the agenda, with job or budget cuts involved, then you can expect all the big guns to come out.

If you are being targeted
Generally speaking, you should deal with this as you should deal with *anyone* who makes you an offer or a deal – ask for more information, and don't trust what they say. Ask yourself what their interest in the matter and their

Typical political shenanigans

actual goals might be. What exactly do they want you to do? Is this in line with your priorities and interest? The organisations? Are they speaking to you in private, and what would happen if this conversation went public? What is the cost (or benefit) to you if you choose one side or another, and how does it fit into your long-term plans?

If you are doing this
Congratulations, you are now getting the hang of office politics! Keep in mind that you are persuading someone, not ordering them around, so keep all of the lessons on influencing in mind from the previous sections. At the same time, you'll be dealing with tough people, particularly at the higher levels of the business, which is where the general information given regarding negotiation will serve you well.

Delay via questioning

Any major business decision requires data – historical trends, current status, and predictions regarding the possible outcomes. But the world is fast-paced and uncertain, which means that there will never be perfect knowledge of the outcome. In other words, business decisions require taking a bit of risk. Even experienced managers have trouble finding the balance between taking risks and taking time to gather data.

Sneaky managers use this fact to indefinitely delay projects or decisions which they don't like. They may do this because they don't want to say 'no' outright, they may not believe you can handle rejection, they may even want to delay you while they steal your idea. Regardless of the reason, they will provide seemingly professional requests for more information without the slightest intention of moving your project forward.

If you are being targeted
One of the first things to determine is whether your manager is really doing this. Some people naturally have a slow and analytical style, one which they switch to under high-pressure situations such as, well, making major decisions.

To start with, you should ask questions which examine their dedication to supporting your idea. For example: what do you need to be convinced? What specific criteria does I need to fulfil? How much time/effort should I create? Who else should be involved in this evaluation? How will this project affect you personally? And what should we consider as the go/no-go decision point for approving this idea?

You should also ask about other, competing projects which may be taking up their attention. Try to find out how your proposal stacks up to the others, and how those proposals will directly benefit your manager. Ask what other tasks you should be deprioritising to provide the extra information required.

As with all discussions, be confident and assertive, but not rude. If you receive answers which make it clear that your manager is never going to support you, then there are two options. The first is to find another sponsor for the idea – someone else at the same level in the hierarchy, or even further up. This can lead to political problems with your current manager but may be worth it if the idea is good enough (for your company and your career). Or you can simply drop the idea, and let it die of neglect.

If you are doing this
This is an exceptionally difficult tactic to catch, which means you can do it often with limited risk to your reputation. It does lead to a lot of wasted time by your team member as they chase down the requested data – but if this is irrelevant to you then it is a simple way to block unwanted decisions. Do be aware that using this excessively will lead to the reputation of a boring, risk-averse bureaucrat – i.e. the last person that management will want to promote. But when it comes to covering your arse from unwanted consequences, this is difficult to beat.

Development opportunities
One of the most important roles of a manager is to develop their team members. A large part of this comes from delegating tasks which are difficult but achievable – stretch goals, as they are usually called. But many tasks are, well, shit. They are boring, irrelevant, political suicide, etc. The manager may not be able to do it themselves, they may need to demonstrate their delegation-focused management style to others, they may even be trying to get rid of you by dumping several impossible tasks on your desk. Regardless of the reason, they will try to sell you on the benefits of the task while conveniently forgetting to mention the downsides. And it will very often be sold as a 'development opportunity'.

If you are being targeted
You need to know if this is a real opportunity, or if you are being sold a toxic project. Any time that something new comes in from your boss, you need to ask a number of semi-critical questions regarding your role and the project:

Typical political shenanigans

- **Why were you chosen for this role?** It's not enough to simply hear that the project will be a great opportunity, there needs to be a good reason why you, of the whole team, are the best one to take it on. Who else was considered? Which of your talents are necessary for success? How does it match with your development plans, and why do they think it will improve your skills?
- **What are the specifics of the project?** What are the conditions for success? What resources can you call upon? What are the timelines, and who is impacted by the outcome? What priority should it have and what others tasks should be deprioritised to make room for it?

If the project is a serious offer, then there should be reasonable answers to all of these questions – and you should be able to create a clear definition of success. If it is a toxic one, you will see evasive answers and deflections on many of the more critical requests, and the idea of 'success' will be something like 'we'll decide at the time'.

If you feel it is a 'development opportunity' being delegated to you, there are several possible approaches. You can simply say no, citing your other workload and more important projects – this only works if you do actually have other more important things to do. You can simply say yes, accepting the task and its' disadvantages – this is sometimes worthwhile if the task is not *that* bad and you need to build up political currency with your boss. You can say that it's too early to make the call and request a meeting to define objectives – this can delay the delegation and may get your boss to choose an easier target. Or you can call out their blatant attempt at selling you a toxic project – this is direct, clearly shows your political knowledge to your manager, but runs the risk of starting a major argument if you are wrong.

If you are doing this

The more often you do this, the more obvious it becomes to everyone around. Your team will very quickly realise that your opportunities are not as amazing as you say, and they will quickly become remarkably creative at avoiding these chances. Save this for the most important occasions, where it is vital that you dump a project on another. Generally this means tasks which are politically dangerous, or where you are fairly certain that the project will fail.

Toxic projects require a lot of selling, so ensure that you plan ahead. Think about the currencies which your target values, and find aspects of the project which match those. Find reasonable excuses for those aspects which you know they will hate, and don't mention the worst parts at all. Your job here is to tailor the sales pitch to the target. Naturally, you should only do this to colleagues who you neither respect nor need.

I'd like to help, but…
The act of pretending that they would really, really like to support the cause being suggested, but are prevented from doing so by upper management/legal/HR/any other convenient scapegoat. Naturally this excuse disappears when a project aligned with their priorities comes by.

This is an exceptionally common tactic, and it's generally considered a legitimate approach by managers who want to deflect an idea without discouraging the requester. You can also view it as the opposite side of back-channel influence – there is always a way to achieve things outside the rules, but they don't like you or your idea enough to help.

If you are being targeted
It helps to be part of the local gossip network when coming up against cases like this, because it will provide names of those who have gotten out-of-channel support. Ask around, find out some details of how they received this benefit. Check the rules and regulations of your company, even the SOP if it exists – you don't want to follow it, but it helps to know what the 'official' approach would be. Know the rules so that you can persuade others to break them.

Once you have this, start a discussion with your counterpart. Ask what they would need to bend the rules for you, or to offer support. What happened in other situations or with other people? What if you found a creative way to get additional support for the idea? What if you asked their boss for help? Are they *really* unable to help you here? These questions are best asked politely and calmly – you don't want to ruin a working relationship over a minor issue. But it never hurts to 'ask for more information', and by doing so you may nudge them towards supporting you.

If you are doing this
There are pluses and minuses to this approach. On the one hand, it allows you to block an idea without openly exposing your resistance or disapproval. This can keep relationships open and allow you to remain neutral on dangerous topics. On the other hand, it's generally quite obvious when

someone is doing this, and you run the risk that they will escalate the issue over your head to someone who *will* be interested.

To avoid this, you need to be certain that those you are blocking are politically naïve enough not to notice your tactic. Alternatively, they need to be politically unconnected, such that they cannot go around you to get approval from higher management levels. These requirements limit its use to newer employees – for the more senior ones you can just explain why their cause won't work. They will understand.

Stealing ideas

There are a number of people out there who will happily steal the ideas of others, presenting them to higher management as their own. The particularly nasty ones will first persuade you that the idea is terrible, and *then* go on to steal it – confident that you won't bother to follow it up. Regardless of the method this is both extremely irritating and guaranteed to remove any motivation in the group to innovate. After all, why bother with new ideas when you won't get the credit for it?

Unfortunately this is very common in the business world, particularly in large companies or ones where there is high pressure to perform. Although blatantly running off with an idea is rare, it is common for managers to say that you cannot talk to Steering Committee Number 24, and so offer to represent you and your idea instead. Naturally, they then forget to give you the credit.

If you are being targeted

The best way to avoid this is to *fully own* your own clever ideas. If you are convinced that your idea is good, then stand behind it. Thank people for their offer of help and support, but insist that you need to take responsibility for taking it further. Point out that you are the expert on the idea, and if nothing else, you can frame it as a learning experience to understand how the company works.

This doesn't always work, because there are some levels where you really can't turn up and present an idea. But it never hurts to put effort into insisting that you should be involved. Ask a few doubting questions to make it clear that they probably won't cope without you: Will they be able to answer the technical questions? *Really?* What are the consequences if they catch you out? Why do they believe that you cannot present the idea? Why don't we become the first team to bring a lower-level manager into the steering committee?

If they've already stolen your idea, then you need to decide if it is really worth saying something. You'll inevitably be working with them for a while (particularly if it's a direct manager), so sometimes it's not worth burning bridges. Having said that, it's usually better to handle it assertively – not only is it better for your long-term career, but you'll feel happier too. Confront the thief, remain calm and rational – never become emotional or you will reinforce their belief that you aren't capable of taking the idea further. Offer a few positive suggestions, and remember that even if it doesn't work out well, they won't steal from you in the future.

One interesting aspect of all of this is that you aren't really *harmed* by the act of having your ideas stolen. Yes, you miss out on the rewards for clever ideas, but it doesn't take anything away from your current level. In fact, you'll find the idea stealer becomes more dependent on you – they need to understand how to implement an often-half-understood idea.

If you are doing this
Blatantly stealing ideas is generally *very easy to spot* after the fact – someone will eventually notice that their clever idea is being implemented, and that they aren't getting any credit. Which means that if you are going to do this, the idea needs to be good enough that you can take the hit to your reputation amongst your team. Ensure you have a plan for improving your position based on the idea, and have it in place before passing it off as your own.

A significantly less-risky way to do this is to give *some* credit to the originator, but make it clear to others that you were a vital part of brainstorming or turning it from 'idea' into 'proposal'. This is particularly easy if you are a manager – your job, after all, is to move clever ideas from the team up the hierarchy. A little bit of exaggeration at this point will go a long way.

Vague promises
This is the art of making a vague promise about benefits in the future in order to get something today. A promotion may be coming, but you need to finish this major project first. A future full of exciting and fancy new opportunities awaits, at least once this year of copying papers and bringing people coffee has finished. There are never any firm promises, because there is never any real motivation to provide the opportunity. Instead, it is a

Typical political shenanigans

simple way to manipulate others into doing things they normally wouldn't do.

The reason it is effective is because we instinctively believe that we will be rewarded for our work. This is often (but not always) the case, and the idea that we trade additional effort for later reward such as promotion is the basis of all organisations. This, unfortunately, means that it is easy for others to manipulate us with vaguely implied promises of better things to come.

If you are being targeted
This is a very, very common management technique, which very conveniently forgets reality – the hierarchy gets narrower as you go further up. The entire team cannot be promoted to the next level, and any attempt to persuade them of this is a lie. You will need to ask targeted questions to determine if this is a real, concrete offer, or if they are lying to motivate you.

It is vital to get details out of your counterpart. Can they be more specific about the offer? How does this assignment relate to the promise of promotion? What happens if they move to a new role, leaving you behind? Why were you chosen for this 'chance' to prove yourself? Who else is in the running for the promised reward? What happens if I don't take this chance?

Watch their responses to these questions. Honest offers will be clearly explained, with a clear set of criteria to hit. Vague, non-committal answers from a defensive manager is a sure sign that you are being manipulated. This is usually a good time to openly raise the issue – note that this appears to be a vague or unrealistic offer, and ask for a concrete deal. You may or may not get it, (and you should be careful to get solid proof) but at least they will be wary before trying to manipulate you in the future.

If you are doing this
This is by necessity a time-limited approach. It can be extended with additional vague promises, usually with some sort of blame directed at higher management, cost-saving programs, or the most convenient of monsters, HR. Your targets will eventually realise that you are not capable or not willing to provide them with the promised benefits. This realisation will only happen *after* the project finishes, however, which makes it useful for boosting motivation on long-term projects.

Once this point is reached, they will no longer co-operate and will often quit. This means that you should only do it to workers who are not all that competent – those who you could replace fairly easily and who would never reach the next step anyway.

Nasty betrayals

Some tricks are slightly nastier, and tend to be used as a deliberate attack on others in the organisation. Although rare, being hit by one of these can be devastating for your project and plans.

Forgetting to invite others

This is the art of leaving specific people off the distribution list so that they miss out on important information or important invitations. This can happen for many reasons – it may be to prevent them presenting an alternative viewpoint, to withhold key information, to sideline their agenda or weaken the agenda held by another that the forgotten one would support. It may even be simple jealousy, as the forgotten person has a tendency to shine brighter than others hope.

Keep in mind that this is not always a political shenanigan. Most organisations are flooded with emails going back and forth, matrix responsibilities are everywhere. It is quite possible, and indeed often likely, that those sending emails will forget to keep you in the loop every so often. This is sporadic and thus acceptable. The problem starts when it is done deliberately.

If you are being targeted

Determining that this is actually deliberate is difficult – a one-off is an easy mistake to make, after all. So your first step is to clearly look at the facts of the matter. Has this happened before? Could they have an agenda behind leaving you off the list? Could it have an innocent reason, rather than malicious? What else do I need to find out to be certain?

If you become certain that they *are* doing it purposefully, it's time to plan your response. First, is it worth getting involved? Or is it easier to simply ignore the situation? What would be the best time to confront them? What excuses will they likely use, and what are my responses? How can I encourage them to speak openly to me?

Once you've figured this out, it's time to meet up and start smacking them with some difficult questions. Why were you left off the list? What is the process for determining who gets information or invites? As this has happened several times, what do they think the root cause is? What will they do to ensure it doesn't happen again? Feel free to go on the offensive here,

Typical political shenanigans

as their most likely defence ("it was a mistake!") can be twisted to make them appear incompetent. In other words, you have a significant degree of leverage, and should use it to get concessions from their side.

If you are doing this
This is an easy trick to sneak under the radar – emails are common, the required mailing lists are long and easily mistyped. It is quite simple to claim that you made a mistake in not inviting Manager X to your meeting. Nor will you usually face any backlash from this, unless it is particularly obvious that they *should* have been at the meeting.

A more subtle variation of this is to invite key players in a decision, but then forget to invite those who support those key players. It is difficult to argue a point when you are the only one in favour of it, and limiting the meeting to your supporters (plus your opponent) can give you a significant advantage in the discussions.

Setting them up for a fall
Projects fail all the time in the business world. Perhaps they were aiming too high, perhaps they never had enough resources, perhaps they hit a stroke of bad luck which kills them before they can reach self-sufficiency. Whatever the reason may be, the outcome is the same – the project will be cancelled, the team will be split up, and someone will get blamed.

In an ideal world management will accept failure as a normal part of trying new ideas. We are not living in an ideal world, and so inevitably the project lead will take the fall – even if the failure was not their fault. Which means that there is an incredible incentive to *not be the project lead* when everything finally crashes down. Avoiding responsibility is difficult, but a well-established method is to use any influence necessary to be moved out of the lead role. This is often to a higher position, based on their 'good work' in the failing project.

The empty project lead position still needs to be filled, of course, and this is where the political victim comes in. Convinced by others that this is a 'development opportunity' or an excellent stepping stone in their career, they move in just in time to take the blame. This is usually devastating to their career.

If you are being targeted
This is a difficult situation to get out of, and thus the first step is to decide if you are *really* being set up, or if it is merely a challenging project. Ask

yourself what evidence you have to describe this as a failing project, and why you were assigned to the role. Do these match with the information given by whoever gave you the job? How much flexibility do you have to change the project around? Are you being railroaded, or is there a chance to improve things?

Generally the best approach (outside of running away to a new role) is to try and turn the project around and move to success. It is vital to identify all stakeholders in the project, and rate their degree of influence and support for the project – who wants the project dead, who wants it to succeed. Try to think of ways in which a successful project could directly benefit those people – this is the basis of your following discussions. Do you have some form of influence which could bring in additional support?

Next, look at the project itself. Analyse the progress, look at the issues, and develop plans. This is important for project success, but it is also important to show your stakeholders that there is a chance of succeeding – and that they had better support you if they want the associated benefits.

Once all this in place, it's time to start doing the rounds of stakeholders. Have quiet chats, personal one-to-ones. Describe the benefits of the project to them, focus on outcomes which are a direct benefit to their power or influence and negotiate deals wherever you can. Start with likely supporters and work your way down to the likely detractors. This takes a lot of time and energy, but it is vital to build support wherever you can. A project with no backers will be cancelled quickly, but one with important people willing to give it a chance can live forever.

At this point it's a matter of perseverance and luck. You may turn the project around, you may be crushed by circumstances. The important thing is to be highly visible in your efforts, particularly to supportive stakeholders, so that they have a chance to rescue you if the project does fail. And if you succeed, of course, then you can easily trade up for a new and more senior role.

If you are doing this
From a purely selfish point of view it is rarely good for your career to head up a failing project. Only in very risk-tolerant or adventurous companies will you be able to spin this into a success, and even then only if you have management support. Which makes it very tempting to get yourself away from the oncoming collapse.

Typical political shenanigans

Escaping requires support from higher-level management for your planned move. Ideally you will identify a vacant or potential role early on, allowing you to request an explicit change (instead of saying "get me out of here"). Call in favours from friends, use the influence of your mentors and network – think of it as applying for a new job, but with a deadline. Your aim is to be out early enough that the project failure is not blamed on you – in practice this is around 6 months prior. Try to take trusted associates or friends with you when you go – you can usually set up roles for them in the next spot.

Who will replace you (the fall guy) is a difficult question. The hands-off approach is to leave this to your ex-manager, which means they will normally pick the next-most-experienced person in the team. If you are vindictive, you can also suggest internal enemies for the role – phrase it as a 'development opportunity' to minimise the chance that they can refuse.

Hiding in the fine print
This is the act of ensuring that a vital piece of information is present in an obscure location of an important report or presentation. The information is there, so the author can happily claim that every piece of necessary data was included. But it is so hard to identify and understand that non-compulsive readers will miss it and the implications.

The typical example of this is a legal contract (where something is always hiding in the fine print), but you will also see this in project proposals and other major documents. There are also many ways of doing it: the key weakness may be buried in a minor section, the executive summary may completely ignore the implications of the facts, the writing style may be deliberately obtuse to challenge understanding, the document may arrive as 'pre-reads' two hours before the meeting.

Note that this is not always a deliberate attempt to deceive, some people are just terrible at communication. But the outcome remains the same – the important information you need is not available.

If you are being targeted
This is a common problem in large organisations, particularly when those involved have strong interests in the outcome of a decision. It's even more common if the person writing the document screwed up somehow, as they will naturally want to hide this.

One way to minimise the problem is to be very clear up front what information you need in a report and how it should be formatted. Read things carefully, not just the summary (this is often difficult due to time problems but you should at least skim through the whole thing). Make sure other key stakeholders have looked over it too – particularly those who you know to be picky.

Even this will not help if you don't know what information you need, the 'unknown unknowns' of the decision. Here it helps to gently interrogate the report author. What are the important facts you should know? What are the risks? What should I know that I don't know? If you were to kill this idea with a question, what would it be? Was there anything in the report which was embarrassing, or didn't support your favoured position?

Watch how they respond to these questions to decide if they are deliberately hiding information. If yes, then call it out, make it clear that you are not impressed. Then give them another chance to provide the full set of information. Most people are too embarrassed at being caught to try this twice, and being generous here avoids making enemies too soon.

If you are doing this
Using this trick successfully is dependent on your audience and the report you are writing. A highly critical audience (or readers with too much time) will go through the report carefully, looking for bits which don't fit together. In these situations it is generally too risky to sneak something in, particularly if there are multiple clever reviewers. Very busy readers (upper management, for example) will rarely have time to go through anything more than the executive summary, which means that you have a much better chance of slipping something through.

Hiding information will cause you many problems if you do get caught, however, and deliberately misleading upper management is a quick way to get fired. Ensure you know who will be reading the report and write it in a way that allows you plausible deniability if needed.

Targeted indifference
This occurs when one person knows that something bad is about to happen to the other, but stays quiet instead of giving a warning. It can be done out of indifference (when they don't really care what happens to the victim), or embarrassment (when they feel that providing a warning is somehow overstepping professional boundaries. But the most common occurrence is

Typical political shenanigans

when people stay silent because they see a personal gain in the failure of the other.

This is exceptionally common in the business world, particularly in large companies where projects die or are cancelled all the time. You will often hear phrases such as "none of my business" or "I was too busy with my work to help", usually said by grinning vultures who are spreading gossip about the failure and its fallout.

Targeted indifference is easy to do and difficult to detect – it simply requires you to do nothing, after all. It is thus very tempting for most people, and you will often see it as a "baby's first political shenanigan" before they move onto more complex tricks.

If you are being targeted

The biggest difficulty here is recognising that it is occurring. As mentioned, it is very hard to detect when people are silent, so you need to look for what is *not* there. In other words, where should you be seeing support, but aren't?

- **Who is not being helpful?** Most work is done in teams, which means that in any difficult situation you should expect to get some sort of assistance from others. Look at your supposed team-members and ask if any of them seem less helpful than you would expect. Has anyone started to help, then backed off? Mentioned that there are problems (openly or cryptically) then avoided providing any useful advice, or even changed the subject completely?
- **Are they really doing it purposefully?** It may be malice, it may be laziness – or they really may have so much to do that there is no time to advise you. Ask yourself why they might be targeting you, what do they gain from your failure? What reasons might they have for taking an indifferent position? Do you think it's likely that they are really out to get you?

Once you have found likely culprits, it is time to force them to take a side by directly asking them for help. Ask questions about the project, its' prospects and what you should be doing. Ask for assistance or resources. See if you can convince them that your success will benefit them. Watch what they say, be aware of signs that they are changing the topic. If they continue to block you or avoid commenting, it is likely that they want you to fail. In this case you should look for help via other routes, or try to find key players close to them who may be able to force the indifferent to take action.

If you are doing this

As mentioned above, saying nothing is easy to do. The real question is whether saying nothing is the *right* thing to do, whether it is regarding your personal values, your teams' success, or even the success of your organisation.

It's important to sit down and ask yourself a few hard questions:

- **Do I have a good reason not to get involved?** What is the cost to me, my team, and the business if I stay out of it? What is the worst outcome if I intervene? Are others influencing me to intervene, so that I will also be damaged by the crash?
- **Do I want to see them fail?** What is my relationship to the person? Are their goals or projects in competition with mine? Do I have a personal problem with them? What will others think if they find out I said nothing?
- **Am I morally ok with this?** Do you feel that saying nothing is against your core values and beliefs? Would you have trouble sleeping if the project eventually dies? And if the colleague is fired as a result?

If you can truly answer 'yes' to these questions, then you are probably justified in saying nothing. If not, then you may want to think some more about the best approach to take.

Malicious feedback

Feedback is important for our development, both in our personal and work lives. Malicious feedback is feedback which is intended to cause problems for the other person – it will distract them at a critical time, cause them to doubt their own talents, or send them off on a wild goose chase. It is a tricky one to detect because it is rarely attributed to the one providing feedback – you will hear that others are disappointed in your performance, they are simply the messenger.

Be aware that malicious feedback is not the same as incompetent attempts to provide feedback. Many managers are simply bad at their jobs – they aren't trying to crush your dreams, they just don't know how to do things better.

If you are being targeted
The aim of this trick is to disrupt your concentration at a critical time. It may come indirectly ("I heard from manager X that you are...") or it can come directly ("I don't think you are competent enough at Y to lead this project"). The approach you should take will differ between the two.

If you are receiving *indirect feedback*, then your first step should to calmly and rationally determine where this information is coming from. Ask questions to gain more details: can they be more specific? Where exactly is this feedback coming from? Why didn't you hear directly? Does your informant agree with it? Can they provide examples of unwanted behaviour? What do they think the intention of the feedback is? And what should you be doing in response to it?

This information helps you determine if the feedback is malicious or not. You don't need to respond in the moment (when most people are irritated and emotional), but can wait a few days before coming back to the topics. If you are fairly certain that it is malicious, you can even describe your logic and ask if this is really the case. Open accusations won't make you friends, but they will make others wary of targeting you.

If you are receiving *direct feedback*, then it is doubly important that you avoid getting emotional and defensive. Their goal is to upset you, which means that any display of anger will show them that the tactic works. Play for time, hear them out and then move away as soon as possible (you can easily say you need time to think over the implications).

Once you are away from the immediate emotional threat, it's time to look at the feedback. What was really being said? How else could it be interpreted? What motive could they have for providing this feedback, and is there any significance to the timing? What happens if I just ignore them? What would be the appropriate response be, putting my feelings to the side?

Your goal, essentially, is to ignore the emotions which they are trying to trigger and go on to be competently dazzling in your requirements. This not only achieves your main goal (extending your career) but also shows the malicious feedback-giver that the approach doesn't work – saving you some stress in the future.

If you are doing this
Malicious feedback works best when given sparingly. If you constantly provide negative feedback to someone, they will eventually realise that your

comments are not in step with the comments from everyone else they know. This will lead them to distrust your opinion and (eventually) to simply disregard it – something which will occur even if they do not realise that you are trying to manipulate them

The counterpoint to this is that malicious feedback works extremely well when it is co-ordinated between several people. One person may be ignored as a grumpy old man, an entire group must have a point. Thus if you want to truly undermine another, find like-minded people to help you out.

Career-killers

And finally come a few approaches which you will see very, very rarely, but which can destroy your career if you do not deal with them correctly.

Terrible option A vs slightly-terrible option B

Good managers try to offer their people different career and development options, noting the pros and cons of each, then gently nudging them towards the option which best suits the managers interests. Bad managers do away with the 'gentle' part, and provide several options which are really, really unappealing, followed by one which is slightly better. The clear intention is to push you towards choosing the lesser of two evils, an option which would otherwise never be chosen.

If you are being targeted

The first step is to avoid getting emotionally involved. Your counterpart *knows* that the options are terrible, they are relying on you responding quickly, without thinking of the consequences. So slow down. Take your time, think about what is happening. Are you being given information to help you decide? What other options might exist which aren't being mentioned? How obviously are they pushing you to one option? What do they stand to gain if you take it?

Once you've taken stock, it's time to push for more information. Feel free to be pushy about this – if they don't care about your opinion, you shouldn't care about theirs. Ask for the rationale behind these options. Ask what other possibilities exist. Ask what would happen if you chose neither. Ask if you can both take some time and develop a better approach. Ask what else they know, and what they aren't telling you about the situation.

If you are doing this

This is a direct method of coercion and (for all that you can dress it up in nice words) even the stupidest team member will quickly realise what you are doing. Which means it is ineffective way to get long-term performance or loyalty from a team – the reputation of being manipulative spreads quickly, leaving you reliant on direct orders rather than gentle persuasion.

Having said that, if you *don't care* about long-term loyalty, then this is an effective way to make others do what you want them to do. This means it is most useful when you will only be there for a short time – because you intend to move positions soon, because the team is a short-lived one, or because you know they will all be downsized soon anyway. If this is the case, then by all means manipulate away. Just keep track of the people in case you run into them again.

Targeted re-structuring

This involves the deliberate reorganisation of a department (or even a whole company) to force someone out of their current role. Most managers who have been in place for a few years have a good grasp of local politics and their role in the company, which makes them very difficult to remove. Reorganising the company itself shuffles everything around, allowing the unwanted members to be booted out, while favoured friends are given identical-in-all-but-name positions to those which have been removed.

A re-structure is of course a very obvious change in the company, one which will be observed by those who are not directly involved. It inevitably trashes productivity as employees start gossiping about the outcome, the victims, the winners, and how they can push themselves into one of the better positions. Bystanders will almost never step in to stop the process (unless the target can call on their help), and may often join in if they can personally gain from the chaos.

If you are being targeted

A targeted re-structure is very, very difficult to avoid if you are the victim. Particularly as you are likely to be the last person to hear about it, by which stage your opponents will have set much of the wheels in motion. Fortunately the process itself is ponderously slow (large organisations don't change quickly, after all) which gives you time to determine what is happening and decide how to fight back.

The first step is to find out if there is really a reorganisation ongoing, or if you're just being paranoid. Talk to anyone in your network to see if they know anything useful. Talk to your opponents, paying very close attention to their body language. Ask them what they know, including the main reasons for the reorganisation and the intended timelines. Who will the decision-makers be, and what are the criteria for making the decisions? Who might be affected? Will you be affected? What opportunities are there for upward or lateral movement?

Watch for shifty answers, and be ready to jump in with pointed follow-up questions on these points. Keep track of your discussions and the information you learn – it may come in handy later on if you need to file a suit for wrongful dismissal. Also identify the "mistake" which you made, as a reorganisation usually follows on from a high-profile failure on your behalf. If nothing else, you should learn from this.

Now you need to decide if you will fight or accept the change. Accepting is sometimes the easiest way – you will end up with a payout, a nice reference, and the chance to go off and do something new. Fighting back is possible but tough – you will need to call in favours from your network and pull in as much support as possible. Keep in mind that winning once is not enough, you'll still find it difficult to progress further within the company. In these cases the only way to truly win is to avoid the reshuffle and then remove your opponent as well.

If you are doing this
Re-structuring is a very popular 'last resort' method for breaking up an established powerbase. The reason it is so popular is simple – it works. The problem is that this approach is a highly visible challenge to said powerbase, and you can expect your target to pull many, many strings in order to win. These strings can reach surprisingly far throughout the organisation – you may suddenly find yourself dealing with high-level management asking questions about your current plans and intentions. Take the time to scope out the full extent of their influence and network, do the same for yours. Don't take on those who are more powerfully connected than you are, unless you can leverage a high-profile failure to pull some of their supporters away.

The second challenge is the legality of the move. Workplace laws do exist, and many of them are written to stop sneaky ways of firing people. A targeted restructure needs to be well aligned in advance with HR and legal representatives to ensure that your arse is covered from the inevitable lawsuit.

17. Appendix: Further reading

Education never ends, and there are no lack of books out there to get you further along the path towards mastering office politics. Here are a few which we have found to be particularly useful:

- **21 Dirty Tricks at Work**, Mike Phipps and Colin Gautrey
- **Crucial Conversations**, Patterson, Grenny, McMillan, Switzler
- **Enlightened Office Politics**, Michael Dobson, Deborah Dobson
- **Influence**, Robert Caldini
- **Influence without authority**, Allen Cohen, David Bradford
- **Never Split the Difference**, Chris Voss
- **Office Politics,** Oliver James
- **The Office Politics Handbook**, Jack Godwin

www.ingramcontent.com/pod-product-compliance
Lightning Source LLC
Chambersburg PA
CBHW070624220526
45466CB00001B/87